RETIREMENT ISSUES, PLANS AND LIFESTYLES

CONTINUING CARE RETIREMENT COMMUNITIES

RISKS AND BENEFITS

RETIREMENT ISSUES, PLANS AND LIFESTYLES

AGING ISSUES, HEALTH AND FINANCIAL ALTERNATIVES

RETIREMENT ISSUES, PLANS AND LIFESTYLES

CONTINUING CARE RETIREMENT COMMUNITIES

RISKS AND BENEFITS

PHILLIP G. MOORE
AND
LIAM F. MILLER
EDITORS

Nova Science Publishers, Inc.
New York

For permission to use material from this book please contact us:
Telephone 631-231-7269; Fax 631-231-8175
Web Site: http://www.novapublishers.com

Additional color graphics may be available in the e-book version of this book.

Library of Congress Cataloging-in-Publication Data

ISBN: 978-1-62100-945-0

Published by Nova Science Publishers, Inc. † New York

CONTENTS

PREFACE

This book examines the risks and benefits of Continuing Care Retirement Communities (CCRC). CCRCs can benefit older Americans by allowing them to move among and through independent living, assisted living, and skilled nursing care in one community. They offer a range of contract types and fees that are designed to provide long-term care and transfer different degrees of the risk of future cost increases from the resident to the CCRC. Developing CCRCs can be a lengthy, complex process that requires significant long-term financing and accurate revenue and cost projections. Once operational, risks to long-term viability include declining occupancy and unexpected cost increases. While few CCRCs have failed, challenging economic and real estate market conditions have negatively affected some CCRCs occupancy and financial conditions.

Chapter 1 - A growing number of older Americans are choosing continuing care retirement communities (CCRC) to help ensure that their finances in retirement will cover the cost of housing and care they may require. However, recent economic conditions have placed financial stress on some CCRCs.

GAO was asked to (1) describe how CCRCs operate and the risks they face, (2) describe how state laws address these risks, (3) describe risks that CCRC residents face, and (4) describe how state laws address these risks. To review these areas, GAO analyzed state statutory provisions pertaining to CCRCs with respect to financial oversight and consumer protection, met with selected state regulators, and interviewed CCRC providers, resident's associations, and consumer groups.

While GAO is not recommending specific action at this time, the potential risks to CCRC residents—as well as the potential for this industry to grow—

highlight the importance of states being vigilant in their efforts to help ensure adequate consumer protections for residents.

GAO provided a draft copy of this report to the Department of Health and Human Services and the National Association of Insurance Commissioners for review, but neither commented on the draft.

Chapter 2 - Continuing care retirement communities (CCRCs) provide separate housing for seniors who are able to live independently, who require help in an assisted-living facility, and who require more intensive care in a nursing home. These communities appeal to seniors because they can enjoy an independent lifestyle with the expectation that they will be able to stay in the same community, with their spouse, as their health deteriorates in their later years.

Chapter 3 - Good afternoon. Thank you all for being here. This afternoon we are going to take a look at continuing care retirement communities, or CCRCs. CCRCs offer three types of senior housing in one location, so that older residents can move from one to the other as their need for care increases throughout retirement.

Chapter 4 - I am pleased to be here today to discuss continuing care retirement communities (CCRC), the risks they and their residents face, and their regulation. A growing population of older Americans is seeking options for ensuring that their assets and income in retirement will cover the cost of their housing and health care needs. One option for meeting these long-term care needs is to enter a CCRC, which aims to provide lifelong housing, household assistance, and nursing care in exchange for a sometimes sizable entrance fee and ongoing monthly fees.

Chapter 5 - Good afternoon Mr. Chairman and members of the Committee. My name is Kevin McCarty, Insurance Commissioner with the Florida Office of Insurance Regulation (OIR). Thank you for the invitation to appear before you today to share Florida's experience in regulating continuing care retirement communities (CCRCs).

Chapter 6 - I am pleased to be invited to speak to the Senate Special Committee on Aging and to have this opportunity to share observations based on several years of research and consultation with residents of Continuing Care Retirement Communities (CCRCs) and Life Care Communities (LFCs) in Pennsylvania and elsewhere in the United States. Thank you.

Chapter 7 - My name is Chuck Prine and I want to thank the Committee for providing this opportunity to explain what happened to me and to my fellow residents at the Covenant at South Hills and to offer some suggestions, based on our experience, which might afford some protection to other seniors considering a move to a CCRC.

Chapter 8 - Thank You Chairman Kohl, Ranking Member Senator Corker and members of the committee.

My name is David Erickson; I am Vice President for Legal Affairs for Covenant Retirement Communities.

I am here testifying on behalf of the American Association of Homes and Services for the Aging and Covenant Retirement Communities.

Covenant Retirement Communities has 12 CCRCs in 8 states serving over 5,000 residents. Our primary contract has an entry fee and provides for modified life care. Most of our residents chose a 2% per month declining refund option. We also offer 90% refunds, but less than 10% of our residents chose this. We also offer full life care contracts in two communities.

In: Continuing Care Retirement Communities ISBN: 978-1-62100-945-0
Editors: P. G. Moore and L. F. Miller

Chapter 1

OLDER AMERICANS: CONTINUING CARE RETIREMENT COMMUNITIES CAN PROVIDE BENEFITS, BUT NOT WITHOUT SOME RISK*

United States Government Accountability Office

WHY GAO DID THIS STUDY

A growing number of older Americans are choosing continuing care retirement communities (CCRC) to help ensure that their finances in retirement will cover the cost of housing and care they may require. However, recent economic conditions have placed financial stress on some CCRCs.

GAO was asked to (1) describe how CCRCs operate and the risks they face, (2) describe how state laws address these risks, (3) describe risks that CCRC residents face, and (4) describe how state laws address these risks. To review these areas, GAO analyzed state statutory provisions pertaining to CCRCs with respect to financial oversight and consumer protection, met with selected state regulators, and interviewed CCRC providers, resident's associations, and consumer groups.

While GAO is not recommending specific action at this time, the potential risks to CCRC residents—as well as the potential for this industry to grow—

* This is an edited, reformatted and augmented version of a Highlights of GAO-10-611, a report to the Chairman, Special Committee on Aging, U.S. Senate, dated June 2010.

highlight the importance of states being vigilant in their efforts to help ensure adequate consumer protections for residents.

GAO provided a draft copy of this report to the Department of Health and Human Services and the National Association of Insurance Commissioners for review, but neither commented on the draft.

What GAO Found

CCRCs can benefit older Americans by allowing them to move among and through independent living, assisted living, and skilled nursing care in one community. They offer a range of contract types and fees that are designed to provide long-term care and transfer different degrees of the risk of future cost increases from the resident to the CCRC. Developing CCRCs can be a lengthy, complex process that requires significant long-term financing and accurate revenue and cost projections. Once operational, risks to long-term viability include declining occupancy and unexpected cost increases. While few CCRCs have failed, challenging economic and real estate market conditions have negatively affected some CCRCs' occupancy and financial condition.

Seven of the eight states GAO reviewed had CCRC-specific regulations, and these states varied in the extent to which they helped ensure that CCRCs addressed risks to their long-term viability. For example, while each licensed and required periodic financial information from CCRCs, only four either examined trended financial data or required periodic actuarial reviews. The lack of a long-term focus creates a potential mismatch with residents' concerns over their CCRCs' long-term viability. CCRC bondholders and rating agencies, which focus on long-term viability, often place requirements on CCRCs that go beyond those used by states in their licensing and oversight activities. Regulators and CCRC providers GAO spoke with generally believed that current regulations were adequate, but some consumer groups felt more comprehensive oversight was needed.

While CCRCs offer long-term residence and care in the same community, residents can still face considerable risk. For example, CCRC financial difficulties can lead to unexpected increases in residents' monthly fees. And while CCRC bankruptcies or closures have been relatively rare, and residents have generally not been forced to leave in such cases, should a CCRC failure occur, it could cause residents to lose all or part of their entrance fee. Residents can also become dissatisfied if CCRC policies or operations fall short of residents' expectations or there is a change in arrangements thought to be contractually guaranteed, such as charging residents for services that were previously free.

Most of the states GAO reviewed take steps to protect the interests of CCRC residents, such as requiring the escrow of entrance fees and mandating certain disclosures. For example, a number require contracts to be readable, but not all review the content of contracts even though some industry participants questioned residents' ability to fully understand them. Also, not all require disclosure of policies likely to have a significant impact on residents' satisfaction, such as policies for moving between levels of care. According to an industry study, 12 states do not have CCRC-specific regulations, meaning an entity in 1 state may be subject to such regulations while a similar entity in another state may not, and consumers in some states may not receive the same protections as those in others. In contrast, some CCRCs voluntarily exceed disclosures and protections required by state regulations.

Abbreviations

AAHSA	American Association for Homes and Services for the Aging
ASHA	American Seniors Housing Association
CCAC	Continuing Care Accreditation Commission
CCRC	Continuing Care Retirement Community
HHS	Department of Health and Human Services
NAIC	National Association of Insurance Commissioners
NCAL	National Center for Assisted Living

June 21, 2010

The Honorable Herb Kohl
Chairman
Special Committee on Aging
United States Senate

Dear Mr. Chairman:

A growing population of older Americans is seeking options for ensuring that their assets and income in retirement will cover the cost of their housing and health care needs. One option for meeting these long-term care needs is to enter a continuing care retirement community (CCRC), which aims to provide lifelong housing, household assistance, and nursing care in exchange for a sometimes sizable entrance fee and ongoing monthly fees. These communities may appeal to older Americans because they offer an independent lifestyle for as long as possible but also provide the reassurance that, as residents age or become sick or frail, they will receive the care they need. But choosing to enter a CCRC can be a difficult decision and is not without risks. Moving to a CCRC generally involves a significant financial and emotional investment, often with hundreds of thousands of dollars at stake. Many older Americans sell their homes, which are often their primary asset, to pay the required fees, and, as a result, their ability to support themselves in the long-run is inextricably tied to the long-term viability of their CCRC. Further, many CCRCs may be financially vulnerable during periods of economic decline—such as the recent downturn—that can result in tight real estate and credit markets.

This report, which responds to your interest in the financial risks associated with CCRCs and consumer protections for CCRC residents, describes

- how CCRCs operate and what financial risks are associated with their operation and establishment;
- how state laws address these risks and what is known about how adequately they protect CCRCs' financial condition;
- risks that CCRC residents face; and
- how state laws address these risks and what is known about their adequacy.

To describe how CCRCs are established, operated, and financed and the risks they face, we interviewed officials from eight CCRCs and obtained relevant documentation to understand their specific experiences developing and operating CCRC facilities. We selected these CCRCs based on a number of criteria, including size, nonprofit/for-profit status, and geographic location. In addition, we interviewed a variety of CCRC industry association officials and experts, including two attorneys who specialize in CCRCs and managers from national financial firms that are involved in the financing of CCRCs and other facilities for older Americans.

To describe how states oversee CCRCs' compliance with financial viability and consumer protection requirements and what is known about the effectiveness of such requirements, we reviewed statutory provisions pertaining specifically to CCRCs with respect to financial oversight and consumer protection from eight selected states—California, Florida, Illinois, Ohio, New York, Pennsylvania, Texas, and Wisconsin—and interviewed regulators from those states.

We selected these states based on a number of criteria, including extent of regulatory requirements, size of CCRC population, and geographic location. Understanding the extent of oversight the entities themselves receive—or the contracts residents sign—when they are not specifically regulated as CCRCs was beyond the scope of this work, and no national source of such information exists. We also interviewed national industry associations, actuaries specializing in CCRCs, attorneys specializing in senior issues, CCRC providers, national and state residents' associations, and officials involved with CCRC finance and debt ratings. Because we judgmentally selected the states and CCRCs we reviewed, the information we obtained cannot be generalized to additional states and CCRCs.

We conducted this performance audit from June 2009 to June 2010 in accordance with generally accepted government auditing standards. Those standards require that we plan and perform the audit to obtain sufficient, appropriate evidence to provide a reasonable basis for our findings and conclusions based on our audit objectives. We believe that the evidence obtained provides a reasonable basis for our findings and conclusions based on our audit objectives.

Background

CCRCs are one of a number of options older Americans may choose to meet housing and other daily needs and especially to receive long-term care, which Medicare and private health insurance typically do not cover and which can be extremely costly.[1] Older Americans may use a number of options to pay for their short- and long-term care as they age, including relying on savings or investments, purchasing long-term care insurance or annuities, entering into a reverse mortgage, or relying on government-financed programs such as Medicare and Medicaid.[2] For CCRCs specifically, many use the proceeds from the sale of their homes and any retirement assets to pay for the housing and care arrangements.

CCRCs are generally residential facilities established in a campus-like setting that provide access for older Americans to three levels of housing and care: independent homes or apartments where residents live much as they did in their own homes; assisted living, which provides help with the daily tasks of living; and skilled nursing care for those with greater physical needs. Most residents must be able to live independently when they enter into a contract with a CCRC, with the intent of moving through the three levels of care as their needs change.

According to industry sources, the CCRC model has existed for over 100 years, starting with religious and fraternal organizations that provided care for older Americans who turned over their homes and assets to those organizations. As of July 2009, some 1,861 individual CCRCs existed in the United States, most of them nonprofit organizations.

Over the last 2 decades, the CCRC industry has grown and diversified, with religious, fraternal, nonprofit, and for-profit entities operating CCRCs of various sizes that have different structures, residential and care choices, and payment options.

CCRCs are primarily regulated by states rather than by the federal government. State CCRC regulation developed over time and in some instances grew out of the need to address financial and consumer protection issues, including insolvency, which arose in the CCRC industry in the 1970s and 1980s. States generally license CCRC providers, monitor and oversee their financial condition, and have regulatory provisions designed to inform and protect consumers.

The U.S. Department of Health and Human Services (HHS) provides oversight of nursing facilities that are commonly part of CCRCs, but this oversight focuses on the quality of care and safety of residents in those facilities that receive payments under the Medicare and Medicaid programs.

While states primarily regulate CCRCs, Congress has considered proposals to introduce greater federal oversight. For example, in 1977 Representatives William Cohen and Gladys Spellman introduced a bill that would provide federal oversight of certain continuing care institutions that received Medicare or Medicaid payments or were constructed with federal assistance.

The bill proposed, among other things, requiring that CCRC contracts clearly explain all charges and that CCRCs provide full financial disclosures, maintain sufficient financial reserves, and undergo an annual audit. While the bill did not pass, one industry source noted that several states at the time were developing or refining their own CCRC regulation.

CCRCs Can Help Ensure That Older Americans Have Long-Term Care, but Face Financial and Operational Risks

CCRCs Can Provide Older Americans with Ongoing Housing and Health Care Services

CCRCs offer older Americans a range of housing and health care options that include independent living, assisted living, and skilled nursing units all within the same community. CCRCs generally offer independent living units such as apartments, cottages, town homes, or small single-family homes for incoming residents who are relatively healthy and self-sufficient. They also provide residents opportunities to arrange for certain convenience services, including meals, housekeeping, and laundry and provide amenities such as fitness centers, libraries, health clinics, and emergency services.

While residents may move back and forth among the levels of care to meet changing health needs, residents generally move to a CCRC's assisted living facility when they need assistance with specific activities of daily living, including eating, dressing, and bathing. CCRCs' assisted living units are usually located separately from the independent living units and skilled nursing facilities. If a resident needs 24-hour monitoring, assistance, and care, CCRCs can offer skilled nursing care that includes supervision by nurses or other medical staff.

CCRCs typically offer one of three general types of contracts that involve different combinations of entrance and monthly fee payments. Some CCRCs may offer residents a choice of the following contract types, while others may choose to offer only one.

- Type A, extensive or Life Care contracts, include housing, residential services, and amenities—including unlimited use of health care services—at little or no increase in monthly fees as a resident moves from independent living to assisted living, and, if needed, to nursing care. Type A contracts generally feature substantial entrance fees but may be attractive because monthly payments do not increase substantially as residents move through the different levels of care. As a result, CCRCs absorb the risk of any increases in the cost of providing health and long-term care to residents with these contracts.

- Type B, or modified contracts, often have lower monthly fees than Type A contracts, and include the same housing and residential amenities as Type A contracts. However, only some health care services are included in the initial monthly fee. When a resident's needs exceed those services, the fees increase to market rates. For example, a resident may receive 30, 60, or 90 days of assisted living or nursing care without an increased charge. Thereafter, residents would pay the market daily rate or a discounted daily rate—as determined by the CCRC—for all assisted living or nursing care required and face the risk of having to pay high costs for needed care.
- Type C, or fee-for-service contracts, include the same housing, residential services, and amenities as Type A and B arrangements but require residents to pay market rates for all health-related services on an as-needed basis. Type C contracts may involve lower entrance and monthly fees while a resident resides in independent living, but the risk of higher long-term care expenses rests with the resident.
- Some CCRCs offer a fourth type of contract, Type D or rental agreements, which generally require no entrance fee but guarantee access to CCRC services and health care. Type D contracts are essentially pay-as-you-go: CCRCs charge monthly fees of residents based on the size of the living unit and the services and care provided.[3]

According to CCRC providers, prospective residents are generally screened to determine their general health status in order to determine the best living situation. Prospective residents must also submit detailed financial information that includes income and tax records to ensure that they can pay CCRC fees over time. Industry participants noted that entry fees—typically made as a large lump-sum payment—can represent a substantial portion, if not all, of potential residents' assets.[4] Residents must also be able to pay monthly fees, which typically cover housing and convenience services associated with housing and are based on the type of contract, size of the living unit, and level of care provided. As we have seen, these fees may also include all or some health care services. CCRCs use a variety of techniques to determine fees, including actuarial studies and financial analyses. For example, one CCRC we reviewed uses actuarial studies with mortality and morbidity tables to assess the likely inflow, outflow, and turnover of the CCRC occupants. Other CCRCs use some combination of resident statistics, Medicare and Medicaid reimbursement rates, marketing needs, and operating costs. Table 1 provides information on the range of entrance and monthly fee costs for the eight CCRCs we reviewed and illustrates how—depending on contract type—costs may change for consumers as they move among the independent, assisted, and skilled nursing living units.

Establishing a CCRC Is a Complex Process That Involves Several Risks

According to industry participants, building and operating a CCRC is a complex process that typically begins with an initial planning phase. During this phase, the company assembles a development team, makes financial projections, assesses market demand, and determines the kinds of housing and services to be offered.[5] Initial and longer-term planning also entails assessing funding sources and seeking funding commitments from investors and lenders, particularly construction loans and state tax-exempt bond proceeds, where applicable.[6] During the developmental phase, developers will presell units to begin building capital to fund construction of CCRC housing and other facilities and begin construction. Once the initial phases of construction are complete, CCRC providers have move-in periods for new residents, continue marketing efforts to build toward full occupancy, complete construction, and begin making long-term debt service payments (Figure 1).

CCRCs, like other businesses, face a number of risks during the start-up phase. First, actual construction costs and consumer demand may not match developers' forecasts. To attract financing from lenders and ensure adequate underwriting for CCRC projects, developers need to generate sufficient pre-sales and deposits prior to construction to show a tangible commitment from prospective residents. In addition, facilities in the startup stage need to reach full occupancy as quickly as possible in order to generate income that will not only cover operational costs once built but also help pay down construction loans. As a result, accurate projections of future revenues and costs are important as a CCRC becomes operational.

Second, entrance fees and monthly fees may ultimately prove to be inadequate to cover the CCRC's costs. CCRCs generally have to keep prices low enough to attract residents and stay competitive but high enough to meet short- and long-term costs. Determining appropriate fees can, in itself, be a complex process because it involves projecting a number of variables into the future, including occupancy levels, mortality rates, medical and labor costs, and capital improvement costs. For this reason, many CCRCs use actuarial consultants to help in these determinations. CCRCs that set fees too low may have to significantly raise entrance and other fees to meet the costs of care and future capital improvements. Fee increases can take the form of larger-than-projected monthly fees for assisted living or nursing care and fees on other miscellaneous services, both of which can affect residents' long-term ability to pay and the competitive position of the CCRC in the marketplace.

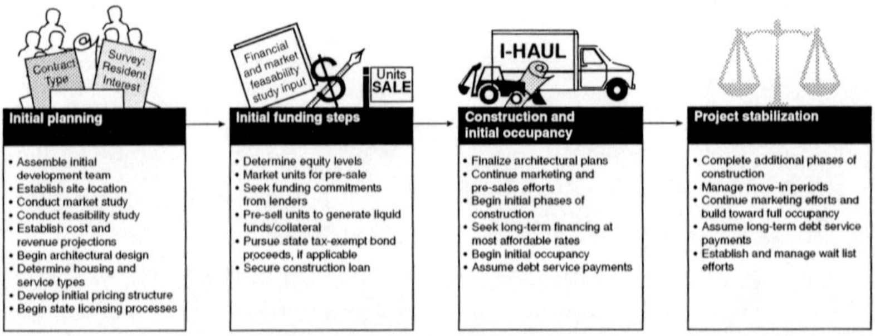

Sources: GAO analysis; Art Explosion (images).

Figure 1. Summary of General Steps CCRC Developers Use to Establish and Finance CCRCs.

Table 1. 2009 Entrance and Monthly Fees for Selected CCRCs by Contract Type

	Range of CCRC Fees by Contract Type[a]			
	A–Life Care	B–Modified	C–Fee for Service	D–Rental
Entry fee	$160,000 to $600,000	$80,000 to $750,000	$100,000 to $500,000	$1,800 to $30,000
Independent living monthly fee	$2,500 to $5,400	$1,500 to $2,500	$1,300 to $4,300	$900 to $2,700
Assisted living monthly fee	$2,500 to $5,400	$1,500 to $2,500[b]	$3,700 to $5,800	$4,700 to $6,500
Nursing care monthly fee	$2,500 to $5,400	$1,500 to $2,500[b]	$8,100 to $10,000[c]	$8,100 to $10,700[c]

Source: GAO analysis of information obtained from eight selected CCRCs.

[a] Fee ranges reflect different size living units among the CCRCs GAO visited, with smaller units being less expensive. The entrance and monthly fees above were for single occupancy. Additional fees may apply for double occupancy, additional meal service, or other amenities.

[b] Agreement provides 60 days of assisted living or skilled nursing care, after which the prevailing rate for either assisted living or skilled nursing services, less a 10 percent discount, is charged.

[c] One CCRC noted that their facility would bill Medicare Part A, Medicare Advantage plans, or any other available insurance for any qualified skilled nursing stays before billing the resident for nursing care, when available.

CCRCs may face other financial risks, including unforeseen events that lead to higher-than-expected costs. For example, many nonprofit CCRCs rely on property tax exemptions when estimating CCRC costs and developing CCRC projects. According to industry associations and a state regulator, however, difficult economic times are causing some municipalities to look for new sources of revenue, and some may be reevaluating property tax exemptions previously granted to CCRCs. Loss of these exemptions can be very costly; for example, industry participants attributed one recent CCRC failure in Pennsylvania in part to the loss of its property tax exemption.

Established CCRCs Face Risks from Low Occupancy Levels and Challenging Market Conditions

Once operational, CCRCs generally depend on high occupancy rates to remain financially viable in the long term and may be at risk if occupancy levels drop below certain levels. Several industry participants—including actuaries, CCRC managers, and industry groups—noted that high occupancy and the ability to quickly fill vacancies is necessary for CCRCs to fund general operations, build financial reserves, including reserves to satisfy refund obligations with respect to entrance fees, when applicable. CCRCs' general operational model depends on having residents enter independent living units and pay entrance and monthly fees. The often large entrance fees can help CCRCs maintain cash reserves, and the monthly fees collected from independent living residents—whose cost to the CCRC is generally lower—help subsidize care for residents who require assisted living or nursing care. CCRCs also rely on high occupancy levels and the ability to quickly fill vacancies to help finance refunds of entrance fees, which under some contracts may be required when a resident vacates a unit.[7]

These refunds represent substantial financial obligations that CCRCs must meet and can significantly affect operations because fees are used to maintain a certain level of liquidity, or cash on hand. CCRC officials said that refunds were usually contingent on having a new resident move into the vacated unit and that a recent reduction in occupancy levels has meant former residents and their families have had to wait longer for refunds. For example, some CCRC officials noted that due to real estate market and other factors, refunds are taking several months longer than during stronger market conditions.

ERICKSON RETIREMENT COMMUNITIES

Erickson Retirement Communities was one of the largest CCRC developers. Typically it built a large non-profit CCRC facilities, each with 1,500 to 2,000 units, for middle-income residents. Erickson established a construction firm to build CCRCs and a management company to help operate its facilities. Another part of Erickson's CCRC business model generally involved leasing the land and facilities it developed to separate independent, non-profit CCRCs, which it created. These non-profits would then often eventually end up purchasing the CCRC facilities. As of February 2010, Erickson had developed 18 CCRCs that provided homes and services to approximately 22,000 residents.

Erickson, however, filed for bankruptcy in 2009. Like many CCRCs, Erickson used construction loans and other financing instruments to meet the considerable cost of building CCRC facilities and ready them for occupancy by older Americans. According to Erickson officials, a number of conditions contributed to their financial challenges and bankruptcy filing. Declining economic and real estate conditions slowed the demand for and purchase of CCRC units and challenged Erickson's ability to raise revenue needed to develop CCRCs. Simultaneously, tightening credit markets reduced or eliminated Erickson's ability to access new sources of capital or to restructure or refinance existing loan arrangements. These conditions prevented Erickson from meeting debt service and other CCRC expenses and led to its bankruptcy filing. Ultimately, Erickson emerged from bankruptcy with a new owner, Redwood LLC, in May 2010. Despite the ownership change, Erickson officials do not expect any CCRC residents' contracts or living conditions to be impacted, as those contracts were with the CCRCs themselves, which were not part of the bankruptcy filing.

CCRCs also face risks from external economic factors that are out of their control and could adversely affect occupancy levels and financial condition. First, slow real estate markets, such as those of the last several years, can make it very difficult for older Americans to sell their homes to pay CCRC entrance fees. As a result, according to CCRC providers, occupancy levels at many CCRCs have fallen over the past several years. In addition, because older Americans may be staying in their homes longer and thus moving into CCRCs at a higher age, residents may spend less time in independent living units than they had in the past. This can negatively affect CCRCs' long-term financial condition because residents in independent living may help subsidize those living in assisted living or nursing care. Second, declining equity and credit markets, which have also been a feature of the recent financial crisis, can also affect occupancy and financial condition. During the development phase, CCRCs often depend on access to credit in order to complete construction, and reduced access to funds can be problematic. For example, CCRC and state regulatory officials suggested that tightening credit and real estate markets, combined with Erickson Retirement Communities' reliance on borrowed funds, were the primary financial challenges that resulted in Erickson's 2009 filing for bankruptcy protection (see sidebar on Erickson Retirement Communities). In addition, occupancy can depend on CCRCs' ability to remain attractive to new residents by maintaining and upgrading their facilities. While the ability to maintain and upgrade facilities depends in part on long-range planning, it can also depend on access to credit. CCRC officials said that over the last several years the availability of both state financing and commercial bank financing had diminished due to tightened credit markets.[8]

Although few CCRCs have closed or declared bankruptcy over the last 20 years, recent economic conditions have negatively affected the financial condition of many facilities and highlighted some of the risks that they face. One rating firm, which produces an annual industry outlook for CCRCs, said the outlook for CCRCs in 2009 and into 2010 is negative because of their declining liquidity and other financial ratios, tightening financial markets, and difficult real estate markets. The firm also noted, however, that the negative effect of the slow real estate market and falling occupancy levels could be softened somewhat by some favorable factors, including strong demand for entrance into CCRCs, effective management practices, and favorable labor costs.

States We Reviewed Varied in the Extent to Which They Ensured CCRCs Address Risks to Their Financial Viability

States We Reviewed Generally Used Similar Licensing Requirements, but Some Required More Information than Others

To help ensure that CCRCs address the risks they face during their start-up period, seven of the eight states we reviewed used a similar application and licensing process. For example, these seven states required CCRC providers to submit detailed financial information on CCRC projects for review by regulators. Most states we reviewed also required financial feasibility studies as part of the licensing process.[9] These studies included projected income and expense information, alternative pricing structures, and, for CCRCs planning to charge entrance fees, estimates of the CCRCs' ability to resell its units that are based on actuarial assumptions.

Among the states we reviewed that license CCRCs, some required more information from CCRCs than others. For example, California, Florida, and New York required CCRCs to conduct and provide a market study as part of its application for licensing, while others—Illinois, Pennsylvania, and Wisconsin—did not.[10] Such studies can include descriptions of the market area and targeted consumers as well as projections of how long it might take the CCRC to reach a stable occupancy level. Pennsylvania required CCRCs to provide a market study only if one was being conducted to help obtain project financing. One state we reviewed—New York—required CCRC providers that offer Type A or B contracts to conduct an actuarial study during the licensing process to help project long-term expenses and revenues and help regulators assess financial viability over time.

States We Reviewed Varied in Their Efforts to Ensure That CCRCs Addressed Risks to Their Operations, with Some Focusing More on Long-Term Viability than Others

To help ensure that CCRCs addressed risks to their operations, states we reviewed generally required that CCRCs periodically submit financial information, but the type of information required and what they did with it varied. Of the states we reviewed that license and oversee CCRCs, most required CCRCs to submit audited financial statements each year to demonstrate their basic financial health, including balance sheet, income, and cash flow information. These statements generally reflect financial performance for the past year and provide a financial snapshot of a point in time, and are not assessments of longer-term financial trends or financial stability.

To help ensure that CCRCs addressed risks to their long-term viability, a few states we reviewed required periodic actuarial studies, but the others did not. In particular, California, New York, and Texas required periodic actuarial studies, but only for CCRCs that offered contracts which incur long-term liabilities by guaranteeing health care services over the long term.[11] One state we reviewed—Florida—did not require periodic actuarial studies but did analyze financial trend and projection data to help track the direction of the financial condition of CCRCs over time. Florida regulators said that they maintained a spreadsheet containing financial information on CCRCs dating back over a decade and used the data to develop financial trend information on each CCRC, including trends of ratios related to CCRCs' revenues and expenses. Florida officials said that since CCRCs generally do not go from stable 1 year to financially distressed the next, their trend data enabled them to identify early on CCRCs that might be in trouble.

According to industry participants, actuarial studies can help in quantifying long-term liabilities and planning for ways to meet them. For example, some said that the studies can provide CCRC management with the information needed to make appropriate plans to meet future liabilities and contractual obligations and to set appropriate prices for short- and long-term housing and care options. In addition, some noted that actuarial studies can help regulators identify potential threats to CCRCs' long-term viability. For example, New York officials noted that requiring an actuarial study from CCRCs every 3 years provided 10-year cash flow projections and CCRC information on actuarial assets and liabilities that were critical to understanding long-term viability. According to industry participants, only an actuarial study incorporates mortality, morbidity, and other information unique to a CCRC to help it anticipate and make plans to address risks to its long-term viability, such as lower-than-expected occupancy levels and higher-than-expected costs. Without actuarial studies, they said, a CCRC may appear financially stable in the short term yet still face threats to its long-term viability.

To help ensure that CCRCs have funds available to pay for expenses such as debt service and operations, most of the states we reviewed also required CCRC providers to maintain some minimum level of financial reserves. According to state regulators, the primary purpose of reserve requirements is to ensure enough time for a financially distressed CCRC to reorganize or restructure financing while keeping the CCRC operational for its residents. For example, these reserves could be used to help make debt service principal and interest payments, pay for operating expenses, or assist with difficult economic times or other types of contingencies. Reserve requirements in the states we reviewed were typically expressed in terms of total debt service payments for a time period ranging from 6 months in Illinois to 1 year in states such as California, Florida, New York, Pennsylvania, and Texas. Some states also required a reserve for operating costs that ranged from 2-½ months to 1 year. New York, by comparison, required debt service and operating cost reserves along with an additional reserve for CCRC facility repairs and replacement. One state—Wisconsin—did not have reserve requirements. Wisconsin state officials said that their statutory authority generally focused on the content of CCRC resident contracts. While these reserve requirements can provide a CCRC with enough time to work to improve financial conditions, several industry participants said that reserves are not intended to ensure viability over the long term. In addition, one industry official said that CCRCs experiencing financial difficulties are often purchased by other CCRCs.

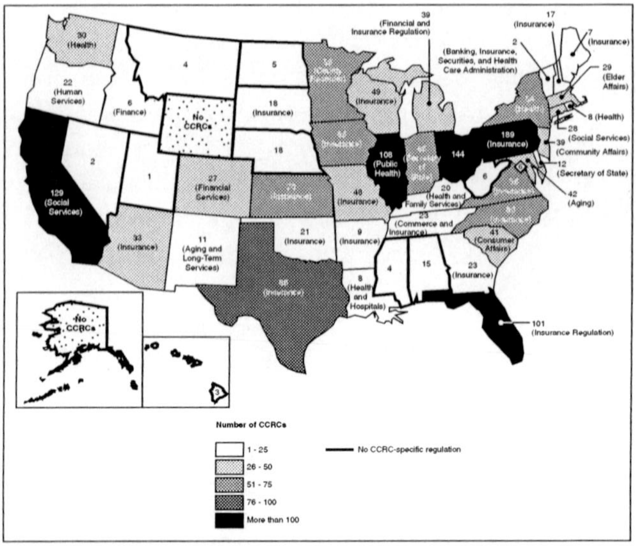

Sources: GAO analysis of CCRC industry data; Art Explosion (map).

Figure 2. Number of CCRCs and Regulatory Departments Used for State Oversight of CCRCs.

Finally, though most states required CCRCs to submit financial information, not all states we reviewed did financial examinations. According to regulatory officials, California, Florida, Illinois, New York, Pennsylvania, Texas, and Wisconsin all had the regulatory authority to financially examine CCRCs to assess financial condition or viability, but only Florida, New York, and Pennsylvania had conducted examinations.[12] Some states also said that they maintained ongoing communication with CCRC management, particularly when regulators had any questions or needed clarification on financial documents under review. These state regulators said that the informal communication channels helped them to understand CCRC operations better than they would if they relied on periodically reported information alone.

Industry Information Suggests Most States Regulate CCRCs and Do So with Various State Departments, but Some Have No CCRC-Specific Regulations

While we did not survey all 50 states as part of our review, according to one industry study, 38 states have some level of regulation specifically addressing CCRCs, while 12 states plus the District of Columbia do not.[13] Among the 38 states that have CCRC-specific regulation, CCRCs are overseen by a variety of state departments. Some states oversee CCRCs through departments that concentrate on insurance, financial services, or banking. Other states regulate CCRCs through departments of social services, aging or elder services, or community affairs. Figure 2 provides information as of 2009 on the states that specifically regulate CCRCs, the type of department with oversight responsibility, and the number of CCRCs in each state.[14] In addition, all nursing homes—including those that are part of a CCRC—are subject to federal oversight if they participate in Medicare or Medicaid programs.[15] Because some states do not appear to have CCRC-specific regulations, an entity in one state might be licensed and regulated as a CCRC while a similar entity in another state may not. While we did not review laws and regulations in the states that did not appear to have specific CCRC regulations, to the extent that states do not license CCRCs and oversee their contracts, residents in those states may not receive the same protections as CCRC residents in states with such regulations. One of the eight states we reviewed—Ohio—did not specifically license or regulate CCRCs. However, an industry official from Ohio said the separate components of CCRCs operating within that state are generally regulated as if they were stand-alone entities. For example, Ohio's Department of Health regulates assisted living and nursing home facilities. In prior work that also looked at the regulation of financial contracts across states, we have pointed out the importance of ensuring that consumers entering similar contracts receive similar regulatory protections across states. That work, which was designed to provide insights for the development of a federal financial services regulatory framework, also highlighted the importance of, among other things, providing consistent consumer protections in similar situations and ensuring consumers receive useful information and disclosures.[16] In a recent report looking at regulation of the insurance industry, a function carried out by the states, we pointed out the importance of state regulation supporting the goals of this framework.[17]

Debt-Related Requirements and Accreditation Standards Generally Exceed Those of State Regulators and Often Focus on Long-Term Viability

When CCRCs obtain financing through debt instruments such as loans or bonds, creditors and bondholders often impose financial requirements and standards that are designed to ensure that CCRCs can repay the borrowed funds. For example, state regulators and industry participants said states and lenders require CCRCs to maintain levels of reserves that are intended to give the facilities enough time to meet financial challenges such as refinancing or restructuring debt. According to regulators and industry officials, lender and bondholder reserve requirements generally exceed those of state regulators. As noted earlier, most states we reviewed have reserve requirements that focus on a short period such as 6 months or a year. But a CCRC provider noted that lender and bondholder requirements are generally more stringent and may require reserve levels twice as high. In addition, bondholders may conduct analyses that appear to go beyond those used by states. For example, according to one company that facilitates financing for CCRCs, bondholders might require quarterly financial statements as well as annual statements.

In addition, some nonprofit CCRCs that obtain state-based financing choose to be assessed by rating firms to help determine their ability to repay long-term debt.[18] We reviewed one rating firm's guidelines, which contain many quantitative and qualitative variables to assess CCRCs' credit quality and financial solvency. The guidelines include financial ratio analysis, trend analysis of financial ratios, review of cash flow statements, and the use of recent actuarial studies for CCRCs offering Type A contracts as well as certain qualitative factors—such as strength of management and governance—to make assessments about long-term viability. Officials from the rating firm noted that their metrics were more focused on CCRCs' ability to pay on their bond obligations over the long term.

Some CCRCs may also choose to become accredited by an independent organization. As of April 2010, 300 CCRCs had become accredited by the Continuing Care Accreditation Commission (CCAC), according to a commission official.[19] Accreditation involves an initial review that assesses CCRCs on an extensive set of standards. For example, the financial aspects of the accreditation process include analyses of many financial ratios, including profitability, liquidity, and capital structure, to assess a CCRC's financial solvency, identify trends, and compare them to industry benchmarks. While accreditation standards do not require periodic actuarial studies, according to CCAC officials CCRCs are expected to use actuarial and other information to appropriately set their fees. Two CCRC providers and accreditation officials suggested CCAC's standards represent best practices and guidelines for CCRCs and they help to assess short- and long-term financial stability.

Regulators and Industry Participants Held Different Views on the Effectiveness of State Financial Oversight of CCRCs

State regulators from the eight states we reviewed generally reported that their regulations and regulatory efforts were adequate to properly oversee the financial condition of CCRCs. Some suggested that the small number of CCRCs that were financially distressed, insolvent, or had filed for bankruptcy pointed to the adequacy of state regulatory oversight. In addition, officials from one state noted that they periodically review audited financial statements and other required information, and have the authority to do on-site inspections of CCRCs' books and records. However, they noted that audited financial statements generally do not contain information that would cause further review through inspection. One state agency had broader statutory authority but an official there said that financially regulating CCRCs was not their central mission. Another state official commented that they lacked the staffing resources to do more than review audited financial statements.

Officials from one residents' association we spoke to expressed concerns about the overall financial condition of CCRCs and how it affects their housing and care, while another believed regulatory requirements were generally adequate. Residents' association officials who expressed concerns said regulators needed to provide more overall financial oversight to compensate for the short-term focus that most CCRCs have on their financial solvency. They said that most CCRCs tended to emphasize the availability of liquid assets to cover operating costs such as debt servicing as the most significant indicator of financial health. The officials noted that this approach emphasized short-term liquidity and current asset and liability information and did not sufficiently consider long-term liquidity, liabilities, capital planning, and budgeting. Another state residents' association official provided a different view and said that its state statute established strict financial requirements that helped discourage speculative CCRC operators from entering the market and encouraged long-term stability in the state's CCRC market.

CCRC providers did not convey strong positive or negative views about the strength or effectiveness of CCRC regulation but did provide various insights. One CCRC provider said that the extent and effectiveness of regulators' financial oversight of CCRCs varied from state to state but noted that for oversight to be effective, states would need specific expertise. The provider also felt that state agencies that had devoted few resources to CCRC oversight might lack the requisite expertise. Another CCRC provider said its state regulator required each provider to annually submit a report containing a number of financial indicators and expressed hope that the regulator would use the data to create a database to monitor financial trends. The provider said that the statutes were adequate, noting that few CCRCs had failed in their state. By contrast, actuaries GAO spoke with said that, overall, only a few states nationwide were appropriately using actuarial studies to assess CCRC providers and that many states were using very little actuarial information for financial oversight. Actuaries said this situation reflected the wide variety of state laws and regulations on CCRCs and noted that states that did not require actuarial studies could have a difficult time assessing the adequacy of CCRCs' short- and long-term pricing structures and long-term financial position.

CCRC Residents Face Many Major Financial and Other Risks

CCRC Residents Face a Number of Financial Risks

Although CCRCs offer older Americans the benefit of long-term residence and care in a single community, residents face a number of financial risks in the course of their relationship with their CCRC. For example, residents could lose the refundable portion of their entrance fees—which may amount to hundreds of thousand of dollars or more—if a CCRC encountered financial difficulties. According to state officials in two states and a CCRC expert, residents are at a disadvantage because any claim they have on a CCRC that is forced into bankruptcy is subordinate to the claims of secured creditors; such as tax-exempt bondholders and mortgage lenders. As a result, residents are grouped with all other unsecured creditors, which generally include everyone who does business with the CCRC, for recouping any financial losses in the case of CCRC financial distress.

We identified no national data that would reflect the incidence of such losses, and several state officials believed that they are rare. For example, a California official told us that there had been at least two situations in the 1990s in which California residents had nearly lost their entrance fees but that these situations had been resolved in the residents' favor. However, Pennsylvania officials told us about a financially insolvent CCRC in Pennsylvania whose residents lost the refundable portion of their entrance fees in 2009 when the facility was sold to a new operator. According to the officials, the CCRC became financially distressed and filed for bankruptcy after it lost its tax-exempt status and became liable for substantial state and local taxes.[20] As part of the negotiations to fulfill residents' contracts and maintain services under the new owner, residents relinquished the refundable portion of their entrance fees. The state officials noted that this concession had limited residents' ability to move to another CCRC, since they would no longer receive a portion of their entrance fee to pay the entrance fee at the new facility. In addition, residents' heirs were deprived of the refundable portion of the entrance fee.

Residents can also face greater-than-expected increases in monthly and other fees that can erode their existing assets or make the CCRC unaffordable to them. Officials of CCRCs, an expert, and resident advocates told us that CCRC residents were at risk of having to pay monthly fees that rise beyond their ability to pay. According to some state and CCRC officials we contacted, CCRCs in financial distress may need to increase monthly fees beyond the typical yearly increase outlined in the contract. Such increases can occur for a number of reasons—for example, to continue to operate when occupancy rates drop, to make necessary or deferred physical improvements, cover unplanned increases in operational expenses such as rising labor costs, or to keep the facility competitive in order to attract new residents.

Residents may be living on a fixed income and may not be able to afford these increases, especially over an extended period. CCRC providers in Florida and Wisconsin said that they had had residents who exhausted their assets earlier than planned because of monthly fee increases. According to CCRC operators, residents are not generally at risk of being required to leave a CCRC when they exhaust their assets but instead use the refundable portion of their entrance fee, if there is one, to cover monthly costs. When these funds are gone, the CCRC uses charitable funds, voluntarily contributed by other CCRC residents, to support the residents.

CCRC residents also face the risk of losing their residence and familiar surroundings in the event of a CCRC closure. According to CCRC and elder care experts, closures occur for a number of reasons, including bankruptcy or an operator's decision to consolidate multiple CCRCs and close less profitable locations. Although state officials and other CCRC experts indicated that such events are rare, they have happened. For example, a residents' advocate and state regulators told us that in 2007, a CCRC in California that had lost $11 million over 10 years closed due to consistently low occupancy rates. Several residents were dissatisfied with the CCRC's handling of their contracts and resisted the proposed transfer to an alternate facility, and filed a lawsuit against the facility. Ultimately, they were removed from their residence when the CCRC closed. According to CCRC and elder care experts, residents who must move when their CCRC closes face the risk of trauma during and after the transfer to a new CCRC facility. One resident advocacy group told us that a forced move can be very disruptive to members of a CCRC population, in some cases with consequences for their physical and emotional well-being.

Residents also Face Other Risks Related to CCRC Operations

Residents may not be satisfied initially—or over the long term—with the CCRC into which they have moved and may have limited financial and other recourse. For example, dissatisfied residents may have limited ability to move out. According to an expert on CCRCs, some residents may experience "buyer's remorse" after entering a CCRC if the community, services, or other aspects of the CCRC do not match their initial perceptions. These advocates told us that residents were often focused on certain elements of care and housing, such as amenities and culture, when choosing a CCRC and might not, for example, pay enough attention to financial information that could affect them. Residents who wish to move, for instance, may find that the contractually designated rescission period has ended and that moving will result in significant fines or reductions to the refundable portion of their entrance fee. But these financial losses can limit their choice of other long-term care options that require a similar investment. Residents also face the risk of being transferred involuntarily from one level of care to another or of not being able to obtain on-site assisted living or nursing care when needed. Policies regarding admission and discharge from different levels of care can be subject to state law, but this decision can be a point of contention as well.[21] One 2009 study states that relocation within a CCRC and between levels of health care is one of the most stressful events older adults face because it threatens their autonomy—that is, their ability to make decisions for themselves.[22] Individuals representing various parts of the CCRC community told us that the transfer from one level of care to another is often regulated by state law and that, while residents may disagree with the decision to transfer, the CCRC, in some cases must move them over their objections. CCRC residents generally enjoy continuous residency in the same community regardless of the level of care. However, state regulators and resident advocates told us that while many CCRCs without space in assisted living or skilled nursing guarantee space to residents in a nearby facility for no additional cost, residents can face additional stress due to the transfer outside of their contracted community.

Residents' dissatisfaction with CCRC management, policies, or services can grow out of a lack of full understanding of contracts and related disclosure documents or may result from ambiguities in the contract, according to representatives of CCRC management and resident organizations. Although state officials told us that many CCRC residents are highly affluent and educated consumers, others noted that some consumers do not understand the contractual provisions or disclosures. Further, experts and resident advocacy groups said that the contracts are very lengthy and detailed, containing terms that are difficult to understand and potential ambiguities, and they noted that some residents might not fully understand their rights and responsibilities or the obligations of the CCRC. Finally, a statewide resident's association in Florida noted that some residents have become unhappy with service or policy changes made through the residents' handbook that they believed were contractually guaranteed. CCRC contracts and the residents' handbook are different documents and some residents do not fully appreciate the difference until an issue arises. Further, some CCRCs may impose additional fees during times of financial hardship. According to Florida CCRC operators, for example, CCRCs may impose fees on services that were previously free, such as transportation to activities in the local community.

State Laws Designed to Protect Residents Vary, and Some States Do Not Mandate Key Disclosures or Contract Provisions

Regulating Contract Content and Clarity

According to a CCRC industry study, of the 38 states that have some level of regulation specifically addressing CCRCs, 34 states collect and review the standard form contract that the CCRC enters into with residents.[23] Based on our analysis of CCRC industry data, about four out of every five CCRCs are located in states that collect and review these contracts. The industry summary also indicates that, of the 38 states with CCRC-specific licensure laws, 30 require that CCRC contracts include a provision that confers on residents a "cooling off" period in which the resident has the right to cancel a contract and receive a full refund of the entrance fees, less certain costs. The prescribed periods during which such cancellation rights may be exercised range from prior to occupancy to as long as 1 year after occupancy, and they allow residents to cancel the contract without penalty or forfeiture of previously paid funds.

Of the eight states we reviewed, seven require that CCRC license applicants, as part of the licensure process, submit a copy of the contract form to be entered into with residents. In some of those states the contract form must be approved by the state. A few of the states we reviewed required that the contract be legible or written in clear and understandable language. Regulators from New York, Pennsylvania, and Wisconsin said that they review the contract for understandable language. Seven of the state laws we reviewed also require CCRC contracts to provide for a minimum time period in which a resident has the right to cancel the CCRC contract without forfeiting their paid entrance fees. Such cancellation periods vary across these seven states from 7 days after signing the contract to 90 days after occupancy.

States we reviewed varied in how they collected and reviewed the contract. For example, officials in Wisconsin told us that they played an active role in ensuring that the contract contained the items required by law and met readability criteria. In some states, such as Pennsylvania, staff uses checklists or other tools to ensure that the content meets state requirements and readability standards. Officials in Wisconsin told us that contract reviews there were less structured and that staff generally used their own judgment to decide whether contracts were deceptive, incomplete, or obscure. States can also levy significant penalties if they find that a CCRC uses a contract that has not been reviewed and approved by the state. For example, California officials told us that if they found that a resident had an unapproved contract, the provider would be required to return all entrance and monthly fees (in total, including the costs incurred for services) to the resident. The state can also revoke the CCRC's certificate of authority, rendering the facility unable to accept entrance fees or offer new contracts.

Protecting CCRC Residents' Fees and Deposits

Some states directly protect the financial interests of residents by (1) establishing requirements for fees and deposits to be escrowed, (2) addressing criteria for monthly fee increases, or (3) placing liens on CCRC assets on behalf of residents or confer a preferred status on resident claims on such assets in the event of liquidation.[24] As table 2 shows, escrow requirements varied among the eight states we reviewed but in general mandated setting aside some portion of the down payment or entrance fee for all units in a CCRC. The portion of down payments or entrance fees required to be set aside in an escrow account varied among the eight states we reviewed.

Table 2. Financial Protections in Selected States

States	Escrow requirements– Percentage of entrance fee from specified percentage of units, conditions for release	Policies on fee increases	Liens, preferred claims, or other protections for fees paid
CA	Escrowed funds: 10% of entrance fees from 60% of pre-sale units. Conditions of release: 50% of construction completed and long-term financing committed.	CCRCs must include a statement in the contract that says changes in monthly care fees shall be based on projected costs, prior year per capita costs, and economic indicators.	Preferred claim for residents if necessary, subordinate to secured creditors.
FL	Escrowed funds: 100% of entrance fees from 70% of presales. Conditions of release: completed construction and long-term financing commitment.	CCRC must justify increases in maintenance fees above Consumer Price Index to residents.	Preferred claim for residents, subordinate to secured creditors.
IL	Escrowed funds: 50% of entrance fees OR letter of credit for equal amount of pre-sale units. Conditions of release: staggered release during construction, and, if necessary, long-term financing commitment.	None	None
NY	Escrowed funds: 25% of entrance fees from 60% (or 10% of 70%) of pre-sale units and equal amount of costs. Conditions of release: construction is complete on the individual unit or a maximum price contract is in place and mortgage or other long-term financing is committed.	CCRCs must develop a formula to adjust entrance and monthly fees to be approved by Superintendent of Insurance.	None

States	Escrow requirements–Percentage of entrance fee from specified percentage of units, conditions for release	Policies on fee increases	Liens, preferred claims, or other protections for fees paid
OH	None	None	None
PA	Escrowed funds: 50% of all fees and 35% of each fee for pre-sales, 50% of cost. Conditions of release: Financing is committed.	None	Lien for residents if necessary, subordinate to secured creditors.
TX	Escrowed funds: 100 percent of entrance fees Conditions of release: (1) 50% of the units have been reserved; and (2) entrance fees totaling 90% of various costs have been received, and (3) long-term financing for construction has been secured, but release is also contingent upon the establishment of a loan reserve fund.	None	Lien is attached on the date when a resident first occupies a facility, subordinate to certain secured creditors.
WI	Escrow is required but not specified.	None	Preferred claim for residents, subordinate to secured creditors.

Source: GAO analysis of ASHA and AAHSA State Regulatory Handbook, 2009, and statements of state regulators.

Escrow requirements are aimed at ensuring the stability of a CCRC during start-up and construction and its ability to provide the services set out in the contract with residents. Six of the states we reviewed required that CCRCs escrow some portion of consumer deposits or entrance fees it received and such funds are not released to the CCRC until ascertainment of certain benchmarks, such as a certain percentage of construction completed or long-term financing committed.

Some of the states we reviewed addressed increases in CCRCs' monthly fees or required CCRCs to justify increases to residents. As table 2 shows, Florida requires CCRC providers that raise monthly maintenance fees above the consumer price index to provide an explanation for the increase to CCRC residents. In California, regulators address fee increases by requiring CCRCs to include in every continuing care contract a provision that states that changes in monthly care fees shall be based on projected costs, prior year per capita costs, and economic indicators. New York law provides that monthly fee increases beyond the previously approved rating methodology must again be approved by the Superintendent of Insurance.

According to the industry summary, 12 out of 38 states that license CCRCs have the authority to place a lien or another form of protection, such as a surety bond or preferred claim, to ensure that residents have some financial recourse if a CCRC enters bankruptcy. Of the eight states that GAO reviewed in more detail, the regulators of five indicated that they place a lien for the benefit of the residents, or that the residents have a preferred claim on the assets of the CCRC facility in the event of liquidation. In Texas, for example, a lien attaches to facilities and assets of the CCRC provider when a resident moves into a facility. In Pennsylvania, the regulating department has the option of filing a lien on property or assets of a provider or facility to secure the obligations under CCRC contracts. According to one expert and some regulators, preferred claims and liens offer limited protection; however, as such claims are generally subordinate to those of all other secured creditors, such as bondholders and commercial lenders.

Further, some of the states we reviewed required CCRCs to communicate with regulators and residents before a potential closure in order to reduce the financial and other impacts on residents. In California, CCRCs that are slated to close must submit plans to regulators that generally address refunds and include a time frame for transferring displaced residents to other facilities.[25] In Florida, if a CCRC ceases to operate due to liquidation or pending liquidation, regulators use the unencumbered assets of the CCRC to provide relocation and other assistance to displaced residents.[26]

Disclosing CCRCs' Financial Condition to Consumers

States may also require that CCRCs disclose information pertaining to the financial condition of the CCRC. According to the regulatory history and literature we reviewed, requiring the disclosure of information about the past, present, and projected future financial conditions of CCRCs allows current and prospective residents to make informed decisions before entering a facility. Among states we reviewed that had such a requirement, we found that the format, extent, detail, and timing of these disclosures varied considerably. For example, Illinois state law simply requires that a CCRC provide residents with a statement that reflects the provider's financial condition and that, at a minimum, includes disclosure of short-term assets and liabilities. On the other hand, the Florida statute requires CCRCs to file an annual report in such form as the regulating entity prescribes, and such statement must include, at a minimum, an audited balance sheet, a statement of income and expenses, and a statement of changes in cash flow, as well as a list of reserve assets.

The extent of additional disclosure requirements also varied across the states we reviewed. As table 3 indicates, disclosures can include information with significant financial implications to residents, such as fee schedules, a history of fee increases, refund policies, and the status of residents' claim on the assets and facility of a CCRC in case of bankruptcy or insolvency. For example, California requires CCRCs to provide residents with a history of fee increases over the past 5 years. California, Florida, and New York require that residents receive advance notice of any increases or changes to monthly fees. California and Wisconsin require CCRCs to disclose to residents that any claims they have against the CCRC in the event of its liquidation may be subordinate to secured creditors, such as mortgage lenders.

Statutory provisions regarding the delivery and timing of disclosures to prospective residents also varied among the states we reviewed. For example, while the states we reviewed required providers to disclose financial information to prospective residents prior to signing the CCRC contract, five states we reviewed also required that such information be subsequently disclosed periodically to residents.[27] Exactly where and how the information must be disclosed can vary as well.

Table 3. Examples of Required Financial Disclosures in Eight States

Selected financial disclosures	CA	FL	IL	NY	OH	PA	TX	WI
Financial conditions of facility	•	•	•	•	•	•	•	•
Fee schedules	•	•		•		•	•	•
Fee adjustment policy	•	•		•		•	•	
History of fee increases	•			•		•		•
Reserve funding provisions	•	•				•	•	
Expected source of funds for development of facility[a]	•			•		•	•	
Refund policies	•	•		•		•	•	•
Status of resident claim on CCRC assets in case of bankruptcy or insolvency	•							•

Source: GAO review of state CCRC law, and contacts with state regulatory officials.
[a] For facilities that have not yet been developed.

For example, some states require that financial information be posted in public areas of the CCRC, others require providers to convene periodic meetings with residents to discuss the financial condition of the facility, and still others that financial information is made available to residents upon request. A New York state official said the state posts the results of any CCRC examinations on a Web site so that consumers can access the information and compare results across CCRCs.

Some of the states we reviewed performed on-site audits and examinations of CCRCs on a periodic basis to help ensure consumer protections, including the disclosure of important financial information. The states we reviewed generally have discretionary authority to conduct on-site audits or examinations, but some are required to conducted periodic audit or examinations.[28] For example, the Florida regulatory authority is required to conduct on-site examinations at least once every 3 years and may visit more frequently if regulators receive complaints from residents. Such on-site exams may include inspections of financial information, contracts, and disclosures and conversations with staff, management, and residents. Other states said that they had the authority to conduct on-site investigations but had not done so. For example, regulators in Texas said that they have not yet faced an issue with a CCRC that would compel them to conduct an examination or investigation, but historically have exercised other regulatory authority over CCRCs for financial oversight. Regulatory officials told us that the state had relied on documents submitted by CCRCs and has called CCRC management on an informal basis to obtain additional information or clarification when necessary.

Disclosing Nonfinancial Policies and Practices

Other requirements mandate disclosure of policies that may have important implications for the length and quality of residents' stay at their CCRC. Some states we reviewed required that CCRCs explicitly disclose policies regarding (1) the conditions under which a resident could remain in the event the resident experiences financial difficulties, and (2) conditions under which residents would be required to move to a higher level of care. For example, Pennsylvania requires that each CCRC contract describe the circumstances under which a resident may remain at the facility in the event the resident has financial difficulties. California specifically mandates that CCRCs offering life care contracts subsidize residents who are unable to pay their monthly or other fees, provided the financial need of the resident does not arise from the resident's own action to divest of his or her assets.

Seven of the states we reviewed also have specific, nonfinancial provisions that must be contained in the residential contract or disclosure statement, but these provisions varied, as shown in table 4. For instance, some states not only require disclosure of certain policies, but specifically prescribe minimum procedures that CCRCs must follow while other states require that certain policies be disclosed to residents but do not prescribe the substance of those policies. For example, in addition to requiring that the resident contract describe the procedures and conditions under which a resident may be transferred from a designated living unit, the applicable California statute prescribes minimum transfer procedures.

Table 4. Selected Nonfinancial Disclosure Requirements

Selected non-financial disclosures	CA	FL	IL	NY	OH	PA	TX	WI
Information about the provider	•			•		•	•	
Affiliation of CCRC with any religious/charitable group	•	•		•		•	•	
Summary of recent state inspection results		•		•				•
Available services	•	•	•	•		•	•	•
Description of physical property of the facility				•		•	•	
Copy of the contract	•	•		•		•	•	
Policy in the event that resident has financial difficulties	•	•		•		•	•	
Non-voluntary transfer to a higher level of care policy	•	•		•		•		
Policy regarding admission/ discharge from levels of care	•	•		•		•		
Rules and regulations of the facility	•	•				•		
Policies regarding life changes such as marriage or death of a spouse		•		•		•	•	
Health and financial requirements for residence at facility	•	•				•	•	

Source: GAO review of state CCRC law and contacts with state regulatory officials.

These policies must be disclosed at the time that the contract is signed in an effort to ensure that residents understand how they will move through the continuum of care. Florida and New York also require that residents be advised of policies for transferring residents among the levels of care but do not specifically set those policies. According to an expert, such policies have been a point of friction between residents and CCRC management. As table 4 indicates, some of the states we reviewed did not have such certain disclosure requirements.

Other Regulatory Protections

Some state regulations are aimed at ensuring that residents can communicate their concerns to management and receive ongoing financial and nonfinancial information concerning a CCRC by forming residents' councils and creating a residents' bill of rights. Six of the states that we reviewed required that residents of a CCRC be allowed and encouraged to form groups in order to communicate with management, including Ohio which has no other CCRC specific law. CCRC management coordinates with representatives from the resident groups to communicate information on the facility's financial condition, fee increases, policy changes, and other issues. In Florida and California, for example, the resident councils are the designated recipients of mandated disclosures such as reports on the CCRCs financial condition, and fee structure. Two states we reviewed prescribed a statutory residents' bill of rights and required CCRCs provide a copy of such rights to residents prior to their occupancy.

Finally, some of the state regulators we interviewed indicated that they require CCRCs to provide marketing and advertising materials for approval. One regulator we spoke with commented that claims or incidents of false advertising were rare to nonexistent. Residents had not highlighted this issue as a major concern for consumers.

Opinions Differed on the Effectiveness and Adequacy of State Regulations

Based on our interviews with state officials, we found no assessments of the effectiveness of state regulations in protecting consumers at either the national level or the state level, and state officials, resident advocates, and experts expressed a wide range of opinions on the adequacy of state law to protect consumers. First, state officials and others noted the importance of certain CCRC law provisions. For example, regulatory officials in Florida said that requiring CCRCs to provide financial information publicly through a state was necessary, because without such information residents would be unable to compare in-state CCRCs in a uniform manner and regulators would be unable to ensure that residents had enough information to make an informed choice of facilities. Members of a national association of CCRC residents expressed concern that some state laws might not address the terms of the residency contract, including the refundable portion of the entrance fee and residents' rights within the contract, such as the ability to renegotiate fees in the event of a CCRC sale due to financial insolvency.[29] Additionally, members of this association expressed concern that CCRCs in financial difficulties might not notify residents if states did not require CCRCs to provide disclosures regarding CCRCs' financial condition. Seven of the eight states we contacted did have a CCRC law that required such disclosure, but one—Ohio—did not.

Other experts and resident advocates we interviewed pointed out possible further improvements to state laws. For example, a law professor with expertise on the Pennsylvania law told us that states should take a greater role in facilitating the ability of prospective residents to access information about CCRCs for purposes of making meaningful comparisons.[30] For example, states could publish information about the financial and operating conditions of CCRCs in a statewide database so that CCRC residents could make comparisons across the statewide industry. The law professor advocates that states could publish information about (1) the numbers and types of complaints about CCRCs, (2) comparative information on entrance fees and monthly fees, and (3) instances of the state requiring a CCRC provider to give revised financial projections. Similarly, representatives of two statewide resident's groups said that residents would like to see states require that CCRCs provide disclosures on their financial condition along with an extensive, understandable explanation of the disclosure.

Finally, although state laws differ significantly in breadth and detail, it is not clear that CCRC residents in states with less stringent requirements are necessarily at greater risk than residents in heavily regulated states. In one state, regulators told us that despite extensive CCRC regulation, a CCRC bankruptcy cost residents the refundable portion of their entrance fees. In another state, regulators said that, while the CCRC law is not as extensive as in other states, they are not aware of any CCRCs that have faced bankruptcies or failures. In part, protection may come from the CCRCs themselves. In our contacts with CCRCs, we found that some took steps that went well beyond what the state law required. The Illinois statute, for instance, requires comparatively fewer disclosures than other states, such as California and Florida, and, according to an Illinois regulatory official, does not mandate that CCRCs provide financial information on an ongoing basis. Nonetheless, officials from CCRCs in Wisconsin and Illinois told us that they provided additional disclosures, beyond what is required by state law. Representatives from one CCRC told us that they offered prospective residents a lengthy "discovery phase" so that residents were not unpleasantly surprised after signing the contract or moving in. In this discovery phase, prospective residents discussed their expectations with staff, had a meal at the CCRC, and visited with current residents and staff. The CCRC had also established a residents' finance committee that received ongoing budget and other financial information and gave residents a vehicle for communicating with management. Finally, the CCRC provided a quarterly operating budget to each resident and made other financial information available upon request. CCRC officials in several other states, including California and Pennsylvania, told us they exceed statutory requirements. Nonetheless, because we visited only seven CCRCs in the course of our work, we do not know how widespread such actions are.

CONCLUSION

CCRCs can help ensure that older Americans have access to housing and health care in a single community as they age. However, entering a CCRC often means committing a large portion of one's assets, and while CCRC bankruptcies have been rare, and few residents have lost their housing or their entrance fees, a CCRC failure could put residents in a difficult financial situation. As a result, residents have a strong interest in fully understanding the long–term viability of their CCRC and their contract with it. However, resident contracts and CCRC finances are often complex, and prospective residents may find it challenging to evaluate the risks they face or the likelihood that a particular CCRC has done sufficient long-range financial and operational planning. Such difficulties, coupled with the stress that recent economic events have placed on CCRC finances, underscore the importance of regulators being vigilant in their efforts to monitor CCRCs' long-term viability and protect consumers.

CCRCs as entities are not regulated by the federal government, and, according to an industry study, 12 states do not appear to have CCRC-specific regulations. As a result, an entity that might be licensed and regulated as a CCRC in some states may not be in others, and resident contracts that might receive regulatory scrutiny in some states may not in others. In other work looking at the regulation of financial contracts across states, we have pointed out the importance of ensuring that citizens entering similar contracts receive similar regulatory protections across states. Because there is no federal regulator for CCRCs, we are not making a recommendation for specific action. However, the potential risks to residents that result from committing a considerable amount of money to a CCRC highlight the importance of states being vigilant in their efforts to help ensure that CCRC residents' long-term interests are adequately protected. Such efforts will only become more important as the number of older Americans requiring assisted living and nursing home care increases.

NAIC and HHS Comments and Our Evaluation

We provided a draft of the report to the Department of Health and Human Services and the National Association of Insurance Commissioners, but neither commented on the draft.

Sincerely,

Alicia Puente Cackley
Director, Financial Markets and Community Investment

Barbara D. Bovbjerg
Managing Director, Education, Workforce, and Income Security

APPENDIX I. OBJECTIVES, SCOPE, AND METHODOLOGY

To address concerns about the risks and regulation of CCRCs, we have been asked to (1) describe how CCRCs operate and what financial risks are associated with their operation and establishment, (2) describe how state laws address these risks and identifies what is known about how adequately they protect CCRCs' financial condition, (3) describe risks that CCRC residents face; and (4) describe how state laws address these risks and identifies what is known about their adequacy.

To describe how CCRCs are established and operated, methods CCRCs use for initial financing and on-going operations, and what initial and ongoing risks CCRCs may experience, we interviewed CCRC providers, CCRC industry associations—including the American Association for Homes and Services for the Aging (AAHSA), American Seniors Housing Association (ASHA), National Association of Insurance Commissioners (NAIC), and National Center for Assisted Living (NCAL)—and two attorneys who specialize in housing and health care for older Americans.[31] In addition, we met with officials from eight CCRC facilities. We selected these providers based on the providers' geographic diversity, facility size, non-profit or for-profit status, type of contracts offered, and income or market segment served. We also met with state CCRC regulators from eight states—California, Florida, Illinois, New York, Ohio, Pennsylvania, Texas, and Wisconsin. We selected these states due to the states' geographic diversity, CCRC population size, and type of state regulatory department with CCRC oversight responsibility. Because we judgmentally selected the states and CCRCs we reviewed, we cannot generalize information we obtained to other states or CCRCs. In addition, we reviewed literature and academic articles by experts in the senior living industry.

To describe what state laws exist to ensure CCRCs' financial stability, and what is known about how adequately they protect CCRCs financial condition, in the eight states we selected we reviewed and analyzed state CCRC laws that govern the financial aspects of CCRC licensing and periodic state oversight, and met with selected state regulatory officials. In addition, we met with industry associations, CCRC providers, and two attorneys who specialized in housing and health care for older Americans. We also met with two actuaries, two actuarial industry associations, and members of CCRC residents' associations that work with CCRC management on behalf of older Americans who reside in CCRCs.[32]

To describe what risks CCRC consumers face, as well as what state laws exist to protect consumers from financial and other risks, and what is known about how adequately they protect consumers, in the states we selected we reviewed and analyzed state laws pertaining to specifically to CCRCs that are designed to inform and protect consumers, and met with selected state regulatory officials. We also reviewed summary information on laws and regulations across all states that was compiled by an industry association. We also reviewed examples of CCRC disclosures and other information provided by CCRCs in states we reviewed. In addition, we met with industry associations, CCRC providers, and two attorneys who specialize in housing and health care for older Americans. In addition, we met with members of CCRC residents' associations that work with CCRC management on behalf of older Americans who reside in CCRCs.

We conducted this performance audit from June 2009 to June 2010 in accordance with generally accepted government auditing standards. Those standards require that we plan and perform the audit to obtain sufficient, appropriate evidence to provide a reasonable basis for our findings and conclusions based on our audit objectives. We believe that the evidence obtained provides a reasonable basis for our findings and conclusions based on our audit objectives.

APPENDIX II. STAFF ACKNOWLEDGMENTS

Staff Acknowledgments

Patrick Ward (Assistant Director), Clarita Mrena (Assistant Director), Joe Applebaum, Emily Chalmers, Erin Cohen, Andrew Curry, Mike Hartnett, Marc Molino, Walter Ochinko, Angela Pun, and Steve Ruszczyk made key contributions to this report.

End Notes

[1] Other options for short- and long-term care include home-based care, adult day care, and hospice or palliative care, as well as stand-alone assisted living and skilled nursing facilities.

[2] Medicare, the federal health care program for elderly and disabled individuals, covers up to 100 days of skilled nursing home care following a hospital stay but does not cover long-term care. Medicaid, the joint federal-state health care financing program for certain categories of

low-income individuals, pays for the nursing home care of qualifying individuals who can no longer live at home.

[3] Some CCRCs may also admit consumers into their nursing home facilities as if it were a stand-alone facility, and have them pay the nursing home per diem rate or market rate. Other CCRCs may temporarily admit older Americans directly into assisted living or nursing facilities to broaden their customer base and generate revenue.

[4] In this report, we use the term "industry participants" to refer to those entities with a role in the CCRC industry, including CCRCs, regulators, actuaries, attorneys that specialize in housing and health care for older Americans, and industry and resident associations.

[5] Assessing market demand may occur through market and financial feasibility studies that assess key variables such as the number of older Americans that may demand CCRC or other living options, the income level of potential residents, average age and age subgroups within the immediate market area, housing values of prospective residents, marital, religious, or other personal characteristics, and interest in various architectural designs and amenities.

[6] Qualified governmental units are permitted to issue qualified private activity bonds to provide tax-exempt financing for certain private activities. In these cases, the qualified governmental unit generally acts as a conduit, meaning that the qualified governmental unit issues the bonds, but the nongovernmental entity receiving the benefit of tax-exempt financing is required to provide the funds to repay the bonds.

[7] CCRCs may offer refund options to residents, which are part of some contracts. According to industry participants, these options include: (1) fully refundable entrance fees, which tend to be more expensive at the outset but involve the full return of the entrance fee amount to the resident or the resident's family; (2) partially refundable entrance fees that allow for the return of a certain percentage of the entrance fee within specified time limits; (3) declining scale entrance fees, which involve reducing the amount of a refund by a certain percentage each month over a specified period of time; and (4) nonrefundable entrance fees that are not refundable after a certain period of time.

[8] According to industry participants, non-profit CCRCs may try to obtain financing from states, which sometimes have funds available through the issuance of bonds. They also added that banks' letters of credit have been important for CCRCs because they have helped CCRCs access capital for development and operational purposes.

[9] Texas law does not require CCRC applicants to conduct feasibility studies but if one is available, the applicant is required to submit it.

[10] Texas law does not require CCRC applicants to conduct market studies but if one is available, the applicant is required to submit it.

[11] California requires CCRC providers to perform actuarial studies for type A contracts. New York and Texas require providers to submit actuarial studies for all Type A contracts and those Type B contracts that result in long-term liabilities.

[12] Of the states we reviewed that had examination authority, the required examination frequency ranged from "as-needed" to about every 4 years.

[13] American Association of Homes and Services for the Aging (AAHSA) and American Seniors Housing Association (ASHA), *The Assisted Living and Continuing Care Retirement Community State Regulatory Handbook, 2009.*

[14] Ziegler Capital Markets provided the data contained in Figure 2. For information on the number of CCRCs in each state, Ziegler considered CCRCs to be age-restricted properties that make a combination of independent living, assisted living, and skilled nursing services (or independent living and skilled nursing) available to residents. Resident payment plans vary and include entrance fee, condo/co-op, and rental programs. Not all of the living components, particularly nursing care, must be on the same campus with independent living. Ziegler's definition may differ from those used by states for regulatory purposes.

[15] Nursing homes must meet minimum standards set by the Social Security Act in order to participate in Medicare and Medicaid programs. The federal standards focus on the delivery

of care, resident outcomes, and facility conditions provided by each nursing home. These quality standards, totaling approximately 200, are grouped into 15 categories, such as Resident Rights, Quality of Care and Facility Practices. State agencies assess the compliance of a nursing home to the federal quality standards by conducting comprehensive assessments. These assessments occur on average once a year, and complaint investigations are performed as needed.

[16] GAO, *Financial Regulation: A Framework for Crafting and Assessing Proposals to Modernize the Outdated U.S. Financial Regulatory System,* GAO-09-216 (Washington, D.C.: Jan. 8, 2009).

[17] GAO, *Insurance Reciprocity and Uniformity: NAIC and State Regulators Have Made Progress in Producer Licensing, Product Approval, and Market Conduct Regulation, but Challenges Remain,* GAO-09-372 (Washington, D.C.: Apr. 6, 2009).

[18] Higher credit ratings can improve the terms or reduce the cost of financing for the CCRC.

[19] The Continuing Care Accreditation Commission is part of the Commission on the Accreditation of Rehabilitation Facilities, a nonprofit organization that operates accreditation programs for various health and human services, including CCRCs.

[20] According to a state official, after construction, the tax-exempt status of the CCRC was challenged, and it was determined that the facility was in fact liable for local taxes, which amounted to about $4.5 million in back taxes, in addition to future unanticipated taxes. This led to the financial insolvency of the CCRC, which filed for bankruptcy and faced a need to restructure.

[21] For example, members of one state CCRC residents' organization said that if room in the next level of care is not available, the CCRC contract will require that a resident be placed in another facility until on-site space becomes available. However, the other facility could be some distance away, which could create difficulties for the residents and their family. They added that this had not been a frequent problem.

[22] Tetyana Pylypiv Shippee, "But I Am Not Moving" Residents' Perspectives on Transitions Within a Continuing Care Retirement Community," *The Gerontologist*, Vol. 49, No. 3, 418–27, (Apr. 16, 2009).

[23] American Association of Homes and Services for the Aging (AAHSA) and American Seniors Housing Association (ASHA), *The Assisted Living and Continuing Care Retirement Community State Regulatory Handbook, 2009.*

[24] Escrow is a deed, a bond, money, or piece of property held in trust by a third party to be turned over to the grantee only upon fulfillment of a condition.

[25] State regulators in California said that CCRC closures in 2007 were behind recently enacted state legislation on CCRC closure procedures. Residents involved in one closure filed complaints expressing unhappiness with the procedures and, in some cases, complained that they had suffered trauma from it.

[26] In addition, whenever an order of liquidation has been entered against a CCRC provider, the Florida Department of Children and Family Services and the Agency for Health Administration are required to (i) evaluate the eligibility of displaced residents for assistance or programs administered by those agencies, (ii) develop a plan of relocation with respect to residents requesting assistance, and (iii) counsel the residents regarding such eligibility and such relocation. See Fla. Stat. § 651.117.

[27] In some states such financial disclosure is mandated by statute. In other states, providers are required only to make such disclosure if requested by the prospective resident.

[28] Ohio does not have a specific authority to do on site exams at CCRCs generally. The state may have discretionary authority to examine assisted living or skilled nursing portions of a CCRC, but this is beyond the scope of our review.

[29] Residents in CCRCs that are in bankruptcy or are sold may need to negotiate their contracts with the new owner in order to maintain a percentage of their entrance fees.

[30] Pearson, Katherine C., "Continuing Care Retirement Communities, State Regulation, and the Growing Importance of Counsel for Residents and Their Families," *The ABC's of*

Continuing Care Retirement Communities, Pennsylvania Bar Association Quarterly, October 2006.

[31] We consulted with Mr. Paul M. Gordon, Partner, Hanson Bridgett, LLP and author; and Ms. Katherine C. Pearson, Professor of Law and Director, Elder Law and Consumer Protection Clinic, Pennsylvania State University.

[32] The two actuaries we consulted were Mr. A.V. Powell, Chief Executive Officer, A.V. Powell and Associates, and Ms. Faye Albert, an independent actuarial practitioner.

In: Continuing Care Retirement Communities ISBN 978-1-62100-945-0
Editors: P. G. Moore and L. F. Miller

Chapter 2

CONTINUING CARE RETIREMENT COMMUNITIES: RISKS TO SENIORS

United States Senate Special Committee on Aging

BACKGROUND

Continuing care retirement communities (CCRCs) provide separate housing for seniors who are able to live independently, who require help in an assisted-living facility, and who require more intensive care in a nursing home. These communities appeal to seniors because they can enjoy an independent lifestyle with the expectation that they will be able to stay in the same community, with their spouse, as their health deteriorates in their later years. There are currently 1,861 CCRCs in the United States,[1] and the number of older adults living in CCRCs has more than doubled from 350,000 in 1997[2] to 745,000 in 2007.[3]

Seniors today look forward to living independently longer than previous generations, but they also worry about whether their assets and retirement income will cover the cost of care they may require in their later years. CCRCs provide a growing population of America's seniors with a convenient range of housing, supportive services, health care options and the ability to age in place. Many CCRCs require fairly large entrance fees (some can be in the five or six-figure range) and additional monthly payments. The fees cover housing costs and a range of care and services, including assisted living and skilled nursing. In addition, residents can purchase a meal plan, use a variety of on-site amenities and activities, and receive additional care which they can pay for out-of-pocket or have covered by insurance.

However, these arrangements are not without risks. The CCRC model is particularly vulnerable during economic downturns, as stagnant real estate markets drive down occupancy levels in independent living units, which serve as CCRCs' primary source of profit. Financial difficulties for CCRC providers could place a consumer's investment at risk and raise their monthly CCRC expenditures. In addition, according to the American Bankruptcy Institute Journal, "the CCRC industry is particularly vulnerable to insolvency, and several CCRCs have failed, primarily as a result of poor financial planning."[4] Several high profile bankruptcy filings over the past year have cast a spotlight on these risks.[5]

Furthermore, regulatory approaches and the agencies responsible for the oversight of CCRCs vary considerably among states – 12 states do not have any CCRC-specific regulations.[6] Thus, financial safeguards and protections, such as liquid asset reserve and escrow requirements or certain disclosure requirements for CCRCs, vary considerably nationwide. For example, only 17 states require CCRCs to submit periodic actuarial studies to address risks to long-term viability.[7] In addition, only 294 CCRCs (roughly 16 percent) are voluntarily accredited by the Commission on Accreditation of Rehabilitation Facilities – Continuing Care Accreditation Commission, the only organization that provides accreditation services to CCRCs.

Finally, CCRC management and financial models are complex. Reliable information about a CCRC's financial condition and policies to provide consumer protections may not always be available to seniors to help them choose a CCRC wisely. Because of the complexity of many resident agreements, potential residents need to consult with independent counsel to understand the full implications of their resident agreements and fee structures.

COMMITTEE INVESTIGATION

To better understand what risks continuing care residents may face, the U.S. Senate Special Committee on Aging (Committee) initiated an investigation into the composition and business practices of CCRC providers. In February 2010, the Committee requested information from five CCRC companies about their business practices and how these providers educate seniors about potential risks of entering into an agreement with a CCRC. Specifically, the Committee requested information on their financial health and disclosure policies. The providers were selected based on the size of their assets under their management and the extent to which they were involved in a federal or state enforcement action. The information collected may not be representative of the entire CCRC industry.

Table 1.

	Company A	Company B	Company C	Company D	Company E
Ownership	Publicly traded, NYSE. 33% owned by insiders and controlling interests.	Privately held Limited Liability Corporation (LLC); owned by a privately-held corporation.	Publicly traded, AMEX. 5% owned by insiders and controlling interests.	Privately held Limited Liability Corporation (LLC); owned by a privately-held Subchapter S corporation.	Publicly traded, NYSE. 10% owned by insiders and controlling interests.
Business Model	Develops, owns, and operates senior living communities, including CCRCs, with a mix of for- and non-profit CCRCs. Revenues from owned and leased facilities were 40% and 60%, respectively.	Develops/ constructs retirement properties; with some owned by parent subsidiaries and others by the CCRCs, CCRCs are non-profit.	Grows by acquiring communities with an occupancy of at least 80% communities rather than developing new ones.	Develops and manages retirement communities, some owned, with a mix of for- and non-profit CCRCs.	For CCRCs owned by Parent, operating and capital expenses are paid by operating cash flow of the CCRCs. CCRCs are for-profit.
Fee Structure	Primarily fee-for-service but some using an entrance fees that may be fully, partially, or non-refundable.	Generally fee-for-service with refundable entrance deposits.	Primarily fee-for-service with 2 having entrance fee contracts.	Entrance fee, which may be fully or partially refundable, plus monthly fees.	Entrance fee, which may be fully, partially, or non-refundable, plus monthly fees.

The selected providers represent a mix of publicly-traded and privately-held entities. Together, the selected providers own, lease, and/or operate CCRC facilities nationwide, providing residency and care services for thousands of elderly individuals. However, the operating profile – or the structure and means of owning, leasing, or managing the underlying facilities – varies among the five CCRCs. The financial profile – or the means of financing the underlying facilities and operations – also varies. Finally, the types of contracts available to consumers within and among CCRCs vary as well. Within a given CCRC consumers must often choose between:

- Type A (extensive contract) – wherein a resident typically pays an upfront fee and ongoing monthly fee in exchange for the right to lifetime occupancy in the appropriate level of care without an increase in monthly fees as the resident moves between levels of care;
- Type B (modified contract) - wherein residents often have lower monthly fees than a Type A contract though the same housing and residential services are included, however, only some health care services are included in the initial monthly fee; and
- Type C (fee-for-service contract) – which typically requires an entrance fee, but does not include discounted health care services.

The unique corporate/organizational complexity of CCRCs coupled with widely disparate means of delivering services between each of the five organizations makes direct comparison nearly impossible. Instead, it illustrates the complexities faced by a consumer when choosing a CCRC.

FINDINGS

Because potential CCRC residents often plan to live on the campus for the remainder of their lives, they expect that the CCRC will be able to sustain the same standard of services offered throughout their stay in the community. In order to achieve this stability, a CCRC must maintain a certain level of financial security.

Financial Health

Major downturns in the U.S. economy in two key segments, housing and the credit market, have increased pressure on the financial condition of the

CCRC industry. Specifically, declining housing prices have slowed the pace at which seniors may feel comfortable selling their homes and moving into retirement facilities. According to the National Investment Center for the Seniors Housing & Care Industry, CCRC occupancy rates have recently been on the decline.[8] Further, volatility in the stock and credit markets has disrupted most companies' ability to raise capital or borrow funds to finance new construction or acquisition. The inability to refinance operating loans or long-term debt may force a company into bankruptcy or increase borrowing rates to an unsustainable level.

Despite the differences among the CCRC providers surveyed by the Committee, the resulting financial condition of the five selected companies generally parallels the industry, in that all five of the entities are either experiencing cash flow problems, struggling with debt, or both. This may have stemmed from the drop in occupancy levels among the five companies surveyed by the Committee over the past three years, particularly at the independent living (new entrant) level, negatively impacting financial performance. For example, the cash balances of the five companies surveyed by the Committee appear strained with four of the five entities having on-hand resources to fund approximately two months or less of their operating expenses. In addition, three of the five entities have borrowed more money than they have in equity assets. One entity in particular holds refundable deposits which must be paid to residents or others that totals nearly eight times greater than the entity's net worth.

In addition, CCRCs may use different strategies to minimize their tax liability, which may put their financial business models at risk when state or federal authorities disagree with the CCRC's assumptions regarding their taxable status. For example, one CCRC company creates non-profit management firms that enter into direct agreements with residents, and then contract with the parent/developer company to lease property and provide services. These non-profits are closely aligned to the interests of their parent corporations, and allow them to issue low-interest tax-free bonds to raise capital.[9] At least one CCRC assumed its non-profit status would allow it to avoid property taxes, however the county court ruled it did not, and the CCRC eventually filed for bankruptcy.[10] Another CCRC has characterized its entrance fees as no interest loans from its residents, and therefore not subject to federal tax. However, the IRS recently stated that entrance fees are in fact rental income and should be noted as such in the year of receipt. On appeal, the IRS did not subject the CCRC to additional back taxes and penalties.[11]

Consumer Financial Disclosures

Evaluating the merits and judging the financial health of a CCRC is extremely challenging for an individual consumer without professional assistance. The complexity of CCRC ownership structures is exemplified by the five companies the Committee surveyed. Each company includes a parent-level organization that is represented by a complex organizational maze of for- and not-for-profit subordinate CCRC and other related (ancillary service) organizations. Further, controlling ownership interest sometimes resides with few individuals, such as management and/or directors, or organizations such as Real Estate Investment Trusts (REITs), which themselves offer additional asset and tax protection for the parent organization. While it may be argued that this organizational complexity is good business, it can clearly add to confusion when a consumer attempts to evaluate the financial stability of a CCRC. Because the financial health of a parent firm impacts the financial health of individual CCRC facilities, it is important that consumers are aware of the ownership structure. While an informed consumer has the ability to analyze the financial condition and results of operations through regulatory reporting, audited financial statements, and other financial disclosures of a publicly traded organization, private entities without substantiated financial data may be less transparent to a consumer.

Entrance Fees

As previously described, there are varied types of CCRC contracts in which entrance fees and ongoing fees will vary. Entrance fees for CCRCs can range from an average fee of $143,000 for Type A contracts to an average fee $91,200 for Type B and $97,749 for Type C contracts.[12] For many residents, the entrance fees paid to the facility represent their lifetime savings intended for their heirs. As such, residents may lack the resources to walk away from an unsatisfactory CCRC experience once he/she has entered into the community if the entrance deposit is non-refundable or otherwise unavailable upon departure. In effect, the CCRC entrance fee may prevent many CCRC residents from exiting their CCRC contracts.

In some cases, communities may promote entry fees as "100% Refundable," though residents are often not entitled to get their money back until management lines up a new tenant for the apartment and the new tenant posts a deposit. At least three of the five companies surveyed by the Committee included a provision where the return of the entrance fee, if part of a refundable plan, is contingent upon resale or reoccupation of the unit. In such circumstances, if the demand for apartments at the CCRC community is weak, the community may have an incentive to fill units that have never been occupied before it finds a new tenant for a recently-vacated unit. For example, the Committee has received complaints against one CCRC in California where a down real-estate market, combined with a state regulation that allows CCRCs up to 10 years to repay the entrance fees to residents, give the company little incentive to refund the entry fee deposits in a timely manner.[13]

Similarly, resident contracts examined by the Committee generally did not explicitly address the impact of a facility closure or insolvency on refundable entrance fees. Most contracts, however, did disclose that the resident has no ownership or lien interest in the CCRC property. The importance of this information for consumers is exemplified by a 2009 class-action lawsuit filed by a group of CCRC residents in Pennsylvania against the former owner of their CCRC, seeking to recover hundreds of thousands of dollars in entrance fee deposits after the company went bankrupt. Residents were required to submit substantial entrance fee deposits in order to occupy an apartment, up to 95 percent of which were to be refunded when the resident vacated the unit and upon the unit being re-occupied. However, when the bankrupt company was purchased by a new entity, the new company did not assume the obligation of refunding the existing residents' deposits. Residents of the community later found out in bankruptcy court that their claims to a refund ranked behind those of banks and bondholders.[14]

While many states have some type of law regarding the escrow of entrance fee deposits, the factors taken into consideration for releasing the money from escrow accounts vary widely. Some companies may use the initial entrance deposits to finance development, make repairs, or repay other residents or beneficiaries rather than keeping deposits in the bank. For example, three out of the five companies the Committee surveyed use entrance fee deposits to repay construction loans. In the Pennsylvania case, residents believed their deposits were being held in safe escrow accounts, however, when the company went bankrupt, residents found that their money had already been spent.

Transitions of Care

CCRCs vary in their handling of resident transitions to higher levels of care. In some cases, transfers may be made against the wishes of the resident, if the CCRC determines the move to be necessary. These changes may be associated with different monthly fees. For example, some contracts reviewed by the Committee showed the change in monthly payment to be relatively minor, and only reflecting an increased cost due to the number of prepared meals consumed. Other contracts specified no change in monthly fees if the move was permanent, but required residents to pay for both their apartment *as well as* any fees associated with their new unit if the move is temporary, though some agreements specify a reduced monthly payment or "non-occupancy credit."

In addition, several companies surveyed by the Committee cited that residents may be moved to an off-campus facility if higher levels of care are full or if special care is needed beyond the scope of care provided on the CCRC's campus. While at least one contract specified that residents are not to incur extra costs beyond the terms of their contract if care is unavailable on-site, others specify that the resident has to pay the difference in cost between off-site services and those services the resident would have been able to obtain directly from their CCRC.

CONCLUSION

The CCRC industry promotes the ability for seniors to "age in place" with flexible accommodations that are designed to meet their health and housing needs as these needs change over time. However, unstable market conditions and poor financial planning have lead to financial difficulties or even insolvency among some CCRCs. In addition, choosing a CCRC can be extremely complex due to disparate state regulations, and variations in the type of contract that an individual can sign. Residents need to be aware of the risks that CCRCs pose and consider retaining independent counsel to review these complex agreements. Some of the key areas that a consumer may want to explore include: the CCRC's ownership and fee structures; financial performance and security measures; entrance fee refund policies; protections against involuntary transfers to different levels of care or to off-campus facilities; the extent to which residents are able to participate in management decisions; the methods available to residents to address their disputes and concerns with the CCRC; under what circumstances a resident can rescind or cancel his/her contract; and whether the CCRC is accredited.

The following resources can help potential CCRC residents determine information about CCRC policies, or assist CCRC providers who wish to strengthen their financial planning and management as well as disclosure and transparency practices:

- American Association of Homes and Services for the Aging (AAHSA) (2010). Continuing Care Retirement Communities – Suggested Best Practices for CCRC Disclosure and Transparency. Available online at: http://aahsa.org/article.aspx?id=11621
- American Seniors Housing Association (ASHA) (2010). Assisted Living and Continuing Care Retirement Community State Regulatory Handbook 2010.
- Commission on Accreditation of Rehabilitation Facilities – Continuing Care Accreditation Commission (CARF-CCAC) (2009). Accreditation Standards Manual.
- Commission on Accreditation of Rehabilitation Facilities – Continuing Care Accreditation Commission (CARF-CCAC) (2007). *Consumer Guide to Understanding Financial Performance and Reporting in Continuing Care Retirement Communities.* Available online at: http://www.olligmu.org/~docstore/200docs/1003-202-contining_care_financial_considerations.pdf
- National Senior Citizens Law Center. *Questions to Consider When Evaluation Continuing Care Contracts.* Available online at: http://www.nsclc.org/areas/long-term-care/Assisted%20Living/questions-to-consider-when-evaluating-continuing-care-contracts
- U.S. Government Accountability Office (2010). *Continuing Care Retirement Communities Can Provide Some Benefits, But Not Without Some Risk.* GAO-10-611.

Finally, the Committee has put together the following checklist for state regulators who wish to implement a new CCRC law or update/strengthen an existing CCRC law:

KEY REGULATORY AREAS FOR STATE CCRC LEGISLATION	
1. Licensing	**Example of Requirements/Function**
a) Project financial information	States should require CCRCs to submit financial statements with projections of at least five years.
b) Cash flow indicators	States should require CCRCs to submit cash flow statements with projections of at least five years.
c) Occupancy data	States should require CCRCs to provide current and estimated projections of the number of CCRC residents.

KEY REGULATORY AREAS FOR STATE CCRC LEGISLATION	
1. Licensing	**Example of Requirements/Function**
d) Actuarial study	States should require CCRCs to conduct an actuarial study which projects the financial condition and long-term viability of a CCRC many years into the future by projecting factors such as occupancy rates, mortality and morbidity risks, and medical costs to help determine appropriate pricing.
e) Financial feasibility study	States should require CCRCs to conduct a financial feasibility study which provides the financial components of a new CCRC including construction costs, operational costs, and debt service costs. It should also provide estimates of revenue such as pre-sale deposits, entrance fee revenue, and loans or debt.
f) Market study	States should require CCRCs to conduct a market study to assess market area characteristics and likely demand for a new CCRC in a given location.
g) CCRC fee schedule	States should require CCRCs to develop a fee schedule which determines price points, taking into account market characteristics and factors such as occupancy and cost estimates.
2. Reserves	**Example of Requirements/Function**
a) Reserve levels	States should require a minimum level of reserves that is tied to estimated costs for a period of time (e.g. one year of debt service, one to two months of operating expenses, and one year of repair and replacement costs).
b) Escrow accounts	States should prescribe the manner in which funds should be set aside for reserve purposes.
3. Recurring Monitoring and Analysis	**Example of Requirements/Function**
a) Annual audited financial statement	States should review annually CCRCs' audited financial statement with information about the financial condition of the CCRC.
b) Financial information and ratio trend data	States should require CCRCs to provide current and past liquidity, margin, and capital structure ratios which should be used to assess the financial condition or trajectory of a CCRC over time.
c) Fee schedules	States should monitor fee schedules to assess changes in fees overtime.
d) Financial projections	States should require financial projections that include estimates and assumptions for many years into the future.
e) Occupancy levels	States should monitor the estimated number of CCRC residents or occupancy rate projections.

4. Periodic Reviews/ Examinations	**Example of Requirements/Function**
a) Periodic or as-needed financial examination	States should require financial examinations to be conducted every three to five years to assess CCRC solvency.
b) Periodic actuarial study	States should require CCRCs to conduct an actuarial study every three or five years to assess the financial condition and long-term viability of a CCRC.
c) Market conduct review or examination	States should examine CCRC marketing and business practices, general operations, and consumer issues or complaints.
c) As-needed communication between regulatory staff and CCRCs	States should require CCRCs to provide a status update on financial and operational matters to regulators, enabling them to assist in early identification of financial challenges and risks to residents.
5. Disclosure to Consumers	
a) Financial	The following examples of financial disclosures can help provide consumers with information to better understand the short- and long-term financial condition of CCRCs, which should be readily accessible in company materials.
CCRCs should provide information about the financial condition of the CCRC to the consumer, including: 1) audited financial reports; 2) information on accreditation, if applicable; 3) key financial indicators on the ability of the CCRC to meet obligations to residents (i.e., debt levels and debt service, liquidity, capital for improvements, etc);	
4) financial forecasts for future years, including financial statement projections and actuarial studies; 5) occupancy trends; 6) average length of time for payment of entrance fee refunds; and 7) a narrative disclosure from the CCRC regarding its financial condition, including an explanation of complex financial terms and concepts and an in-person meeting session with residents to discuss and allow for questions and answers.	
CCRCs should provide fee schedules to consumers, including entrance fees, monthly fees, and fees for other CCRC amenities.	
CCRCs should provide information on fee adjustment policies to consumers, including the manner in which increases occur and increase trends.	
CCRCs should provide their reserve funding levels and sources to consumers.	

KEY REGULATORY AREAS FOR STATE CCRC LEGISLATION	
CCRCs should provide their expected source of funds for development, repair, or replacement of facilities to consumers.	
CCRCs should provide their refund policies and revenue sources to consumers.	
CCRCs should provide the status of a resident claim on CCRC assets in case of bankruptcy or insolvency to consumers.	
b) Non-financial	The following examples of non-financial disclosures can help provide consumers with information on contractual, operational, policy, and other issues relevant to the CCRC, which should be readily accessible in company materials.
CCRCs should provide information about the provider and management to the consumer including: 1) governing structure and ownership; 2) names of board members/trustees; 3) history of the CCRC; 4) for- or non-profit status; and 5) relationships with any outside companies for management or other reasons.	
CCRCs should provide information about affiliations with any religious or charitable groups to consumers.	
CCRCs should provide a summary of recent state examinations including health and safety inspections to consumers.	
CCRCs should provide a description of the physical CCRC property, including amenities and services to consumers.	
CCRCs should provide a copy of the CCRC contract including termination provisions to the consumer.	
CCRCs should provide information on financial assistance policies in the event that a resident has financial difficulties.	
CCRCs should provide information about requirements for admission or discharge from different levels of care (i.e., independent living, assisted living, and nursing facility), including policies on involuntary transfers to a higher level of care.	
CCRCs should provide rules and regulations of the CCRC to consumers.	
CCRCs should provide policies regarding life changes such as marriage or death of a spouse to the consumer.	
CCRCs should provide annual or operating reports to consumers.	

End Notes

[1] Ziegler Capital Markets. (October 2009). *Ziegler National CCRC Listing and Profile.*

[2] U.S. Government Accountability Office (1997). *How Continuing Care Retirement Communities Manage Services for the Elderly.* GAO/HEHS-97-36.

[3] Tumlinson, A., Woods, S., & Avalere Health, LLC. (January 2007). *Long-Term Care in America: An Introduction.* National Commission for Quality Long-Term Care.

[4] Peterman, N., Lannan, R., & Gregg, J. (March 2003). "Protecting Residents of Continuing Care Retirement Care Communities." *American Bankruptcy Institute Journal*, Volume XXII, No. 2.

[5] Hilzenrath, D. (2009). "You're Only as Secure as the Retirement Home." *The Washington Post.* Available at: http://www.washingtonpost.com/wp-dyn/content/article/2009/10/30/AR2009103004219.html

[6] U.S. Government Accountability Office (2010). *Continuing Care Retirement Communities Can Provide Some Benefits, But Not Without Some Risk.* GAO-10-611.

[7] American Seniors Housing Association (2010). *Assisted Living and Continuing Care Retirement Community State Regulatory Handbook.* Washington, D.C.: Author.

[8] National Investment Center for the Seniors Housing & Care Industry (2010). *1Q10 Market Signal: Three Year Occupancy Performance by Property Type.* Available at: http://www.nic.org/research/signals/signal1q102.aspx

[9] Hilzenrath, D. S. (2010, April 4). "Charities boosted profits of Erickson retirement communities." *The Washington Post.* Retrieved from http://www.washingtonpost.com/wp-dyn/content/article/2010/04/03/AR2010040305010.html

[10] *The Covenant at South Hills, Inc. vs. Mt. Lebanon School District, Municipality of Mt. Lebanon and the County of Allegheny.* (2008). Retrieved from: https://dcr.alleghenycounty.us/DisplayImage.asp?gPDFOH=vol593%20%20%20%20%20%20%20%20%20%20%20%20%20%20%200000045A&CaseID=GD%2D04%2D028040&DocketType=MOTOR&SeqNumber=18

[11] Emshwiller, J. R. (2010, June 3). "Retirement-Community Operator Battles IRS Over Entrance Fees." *The Wall Street Journal.* Retrieved from http://online.wsj.com/article/SB10001424052748704515704575282362670440450.html

[12] American Association of Homes and Services for the Aging (2005). *Continuing Care Retirement Communities: 2005 Profile, 1st Edition.*

[13] Emshwiller, J. R. (2010, June 3). "Retirement-Community Operator Battles IRS Over Entrance Fees." *The Wall Street Journal.* Retrieved from http://online.wsj.com/article/SB10001424052748704515704575282362670440450.html After inquiries from the press and the Committee, the company recently agreed to refund several entrance fee deposits that were under dispute.

[14] Hilzenrath, D. (2009). "You're Only as Secure as the Retirement Home." *The Washington Post.* Available at: http://www.washingtonpost.com/wp-dyn/content/article/2009/ 10/30/AR2009103004219.html

In: Continuing Care Retirement Communities ISBN 978-1-62100-945-0
Editors: P. G. Moore and L. F. Miller

Chapter 3

Opening Statement of Senator Herb Kohl, Chairman, Special Committee on Aging. Hearing on "Continuing Care Retirement Communities (CCRCs): Secure Retirement or Risky Investment?"

Good afternoon. Thank you all for being here. This afternoon we are going to take a look at continuing care retirement communities, or CCRCs. CCRCs offer three types of senior housing in one location, so that older residents can move from one to the other as their need for care increases throughout retirement.

These communities allow seniors to stay among friends and near their spouse during the aging process, and for that reason they have grown in popularity over recent decades. The number of older adults living in CCRCs has more than doubled between 1997 to 2007, now totaling 745,000 seniors in over 1,800 CCRCs. With the boomer generation retiring, we can only expect this number to grow.

Over the past year, our Committee has taken a look at the financial stability of the typical CCRC business model. In most cases, new residents must pay a large deposit in order to join a community. These deposits often represent their life savings or their children's inheritance. In return, residents can generally expect to move within the community as their long-term care needs grow, and, in some cases, to receive their deposit back if they decide to move away.

Through our investigation, we found that CCRCs are particularly vulnerable during economic downturns. Slow real estate markets can drive down occupancy levels in independent living units, which are the main source of profit for these retirement communities. Occupancy levels for five prominent CCRC companies we questioned have indeed dropped in the past three years, leading to financial difficulties for some. The result is often an increase in the monthly fees, a reduction in the services and amenities provided, or both. Disturbingly, we've seen instances where seniors had to file law suits to keep their CCRCs' services from being cutback or reduced. Residents may feel forced to put up with these situations because most of their assets are tied up with the CCRC.

This is especially true in a stagnant economy, when financial distress can cause long delays in receiving refundable entrance fees, or, as one of our witnesses experienced, the loss of one's refundable deposit altogether. One CCRC company refunded several sizable deposits only after getting a letter of inquiry from this Committee.

While this represents an extreme scenario, the fact is that many CCRCs who advertise their entrance fees as "100 percent refundable" will only repay them if and when they can line up a new tenant. And in some states, such as California, CCRCs are granted up to 10 years to repay full or partial refunds. Such a delay can be devastating to an older couple who has their life savings tied up in a CCRC deposit.

To supplement our own investigation, we asked GAO to survey CCRC regulatory oversight nationwide. As you will hear, they found considerable variation in state regulations, with 12 states having no CCRC-specific regulations at all. Consumer safeguards and protections regarding disclosure, asset reserves, and escrow requirements vary widely, and only 17 states require CCRCs to submit studies that assess their long-term viability. In terms of the industry's internal policing, GAO found that only 16 percent of CCRCs are voluntarily accredited by the Continuing Care Accreditation Commission. That is an astoundingly low number.

The fact is that while CCRCs are a good residential option for many retirees, entering into an agreement with one can pose financial risk. Our investigation has found many CCRC ownership structures to be very complex, and that financial troubles at any level can have real consequences for individual residents. Evaluating such a transaction can be quite challenging for the average consumer without professional assistance.

Today the Committee is releasing a summary of findings from our investigation, which outlines the financial health of the five companies we questioned, as well as their disclosure policies regarding entrance fees and transitions of care. We also included several helpful resources for consumers and CCRC providers. Finally, we are calling on state regulators to beef up their oversight. Every state should be requiring proof of their long-term viability from CCRCs and ensuring transparency and strong consumer protections for residents. As part of our report, the Committee has developed our own checklist for state regulators who wish to expand or improve their oversight of CCRCs, and we urge them to put it to use.

Moving forward, we hope to increase both consumer protections and consumer awareness with regard to CCRCs. If these companies are going to take the life savings of seniors, they need to be able to guarantee they will be around to provide the lifetime of care they promise. I would like to thank our witnesses today for speaking with us on this important issue.

In: Continuing Care Retirement Communities ISBN 978-1-62100-945-0
Editors: P. G. Moore and L. F. Miller

Chapter 4

Older Americans: Continuing Care Retirement Communities Can Provide Benefits, but Not Without Some Risk. Testimony of Alicia Puente Cackley, Director, Financial Markets and Community Investment, (GAO). Hearing on "Continuing Care Retirement Communities (CCRCs): Secure Retirement or Risky Investment?"

Mr. Chairman and Members of the Committee:

I am pleased to be here today to discuss continuing care retirement communities (CCRC), the risks they and their residents face, and their regulation. A growing population of older Americans is seeking options for ensuring that their assets and income in retirement will cover the cost of their housing and health care needs. One option for meeting these long-term care needs is to enter a CCRC, which aims to provide lifelong housing, household assistance, and nursing care in exchange for a sometimes sizable entrance fee and ongoing monthly fees. These communities may appeal to older Americans because they offer an independent lifestyle for as long as possible but also provide the reassurance that, as residents age or become sick or frail, they will receive the care they need within the same community. But choosing to enter a CCRC can be a difficult decision and is not without risk. Moving to a CCRC generally involves a significant financial and emotional investment. Many older Americans sell their homes, which are often their primary assets, to pay the required fees, and, as a result, their ability to support themselves in the long run is inextricably tied to the long-term viability of their CCRC. Further, many CCRCs may be financially vulnerable during periods of economic decline—such as the recent downturn—that can result in tight real estate and credit markets.

My testimony is based on our June 2010 report, which is being publicly released today and addresses four issues: (1) how CCRCs operate and what financial risks are associated with their operation and establishment, (2) how state laws address these risks and what is known about how adequately they protect CCRCs' financial condition, (3) risks that CCRC residents face, and (4) how state laws address these risks and what is known about their adequacy.[1]

To address these questions, we reviewed CCRC statutory provisions from eight states—California, Florida, Illinois, Ohio, New York, Pennsylvania, Texas, and Wisconsin—and interviewed regulators from those states. We selected these states based on a number of criteria, including extent of regulatory requirements, size of CCRC population, and geographic location. We also reviewed summary information found in an industry study on laws and regulations across all states.[2] In addition, we also we interviewed officials from eight CCRCs and obtained relevant documentation to understand their specific experiences developing and operating CCRC facilities. Finally, we interviewed national industry associations, actuaries specializing in CCRCs, attorneys specializing in senior issues, CCRC providers, national and state residents' associations, and officials involved with CCRC finance and debt ratings. A full description of our scope and methodology is included in appendix I of our report.

We conducted this performance audit from June 2009 to July 2010 in accordance with generally accepted government auditing standards. Those standards require that we plan and perform the audit to obtain sufficient, appropriate evidence to provide a reasonable basis for our findings and conclusions based on our audit objectives. We believe that the evidence obtained provides a reasonable basis for our findings and conclusions based on our audit objectives.

Mr. Chairman, the following summarizes our findings on each of the four issue areas discussed in our report:

- CCRCs can benefit older Americans by allowing them to move among and through independent living, assisted living, and skilled nursing care in one community. They offer a range of contract types and fees that are designed to provide long-term care and transfer different degrees of the risk of future cost increases from the resident to the CCRC. However, developing CCRCs can be a lengthy, complex process and CCRCs, like other businesses, face a number of risks both during their development and after they become operational. First, actual construction costs and consumer demand may not match developers' forecasts. To attract financing from lenders and ensure adequate underwriting for CCRC projects, developers need to generate sufficient presales and deposits prior to construction to show a tangible commitment from prospective residents. In addition, facilities in the start-up stage need to reach full occupancy as quickly as possible in order to generate income that will not only cover operational costs once built but also help pay down construction loans. As a result, accurate projections of future revenues and costs are important as a CCRC becomes operational. Once operational, risks to long-term viability include declining occupancy, unexpected cost increases, slow real estate markets, and declining equity and credit markets. While few CCRCs have failed, challenging economic and real estate market conditions have negatively affected some CCRCs' occupancy and financial condition.
- With respect to financial oversight of CCRCs, states we reviewed varied in the extent to which they ensured CCRCs addressed their risks, and some focused more on long-term viability than others. Most of the states we reviewed required CCRC providers to maintain some level of financial reserves to address financial challenges. In addition, most of the states we reviewed required CCRCs to annually submit audited financial statements that reflected financial performance for the past year. However, only four of the states required information that could help them assess each CCRC's long-term viability, and three states had conducted financial examinations. Three of the states we reviewed required certain CCRCs to perform actuarial studies at regular intervals and one used financial information submitted over the years to assemble trend information including financial ratio

trends.[3] Actuarial studies, according to industry participants, can help CCRCs plan for contractual obligations and set appropriate housing and care prices. Without them, they noted, a CCRC may appear financially stable in the short term yet still face threats to long-term viability. The lack of a long-term focus creates a potential mismatch with residents' concerns over their CCRC's long-term viability. CCRC bondholders and rating agencies, which focus on long-term viability, often place requirements on CCRCs that go beyond state licensing and oversight activities. While we did not survey all 50 states as part of our review, according to an industry study, 12 states and the District of Columbia do not have CCRC-specific regulations, meaning an entity in 1 state may be subject to such regulations while a similar entity in another state may not. Regulators and CCRC providers we spoke with generally believed that current CCRC regulation was adequate, however, some CCRC residents' association officials expressed the need for financial oversight that focused on the long-term viability of CCRCs.

- While CCRCs offer long-term residence and care in the same community, residents can still face considerable risk. For example, CCRC financial difficulties can lead to unexpected increases in residents' monthly fees. And while CCRC bankruptcies or closures have been relatively rare, and residents have generally not been forced to leave in such cases, should a CCRC failure occur, it could cause residents to lose all or part of their entrance fee, which may amount to hundreds of thousands of dollars. For example, residents of one CCRC in Pennsylvania lost the refundable portion of their entrance fees in 2009 when the facility became insolvent after a change in municipal tax policy made the CCRC liable for unanticipated local taxes. Ultimately, it was sold to a new operator. Residents can also become dissatisfied if CCRC policies or operations fall short of residents' expectations or there is a change in arrangements they thought were contractually guaranteed, such as charging residents for services that were previously free. In addition, residents also face the risk of being transferred involuntarily from one level of care to another or of not being able to obtain assisted living or nursing care on-site.

- Most of the states GAO reviewed take steps to protect the interests of CCRC residents, such as requiring the escrow of entrance fees and mandating certain disclosures. For example, a number require contracts to be written in clear and understandable language, though some industry participants questioned residents' ability to fully understand them. In addition, not all review the content of contracts. Also, states we reviewed varied considerably in the type of financial and other disclosures required of CCRCs. For example, some states required disclosure of fee schedules and a history of fee increases, but other states did not. Also, not all require disclosure of policies likely to have a significant impact on residents' satisfaction, such as policies for moving between levels of care. In addition, regulations in some states require that residents of a CCRC be allowed and encouraged to form groups in order to communicate with management, while other states had no such requirement. As noted above, 12 states and the District of Columbia do not have CCRC-specific regulations, meaning an entity in 1 state may be subject to such regulations while a similar entity in another state may not, and consumers in some states may not receive the same protections as those in others. In contrast, some CCRCs voluntarily exceed disclosures and protections required by state regulations.

The report we are releasing today acknowledges that CCRCs can benefit older Americans by helping ensure access to housing and health care in a single community as they age. However, choosing to enter a CCRC can be a difficult decision, and is not without significant financial and other risks. Entering a CCRC often means committing a large portion of one's assets with the expectation of receiving lifelong housing and care. Further, the stress that recent economic events may have placed on CCRC finances underscores the importance of regulators being vigilant in their efforts to monitor CCRCs' long-term viability and protect consumers. The potential financial risks to CCRCs, and the risks to residents that result from committing a considerable amount of money to a CCRC, highlight the importance of states being vigilant in their efforts to help ensure that CCRC residents' long-term interests are adequately protected. Such efforts will only become more important as the number of older Americans grows.

Chairman Kohl and members of the committee, this concludes my prepared statement. I would be pleased to respond to any questions.

End Notes

[1] GAO, *Older Americans: Continuing Care Retirement Communities Can Provide Benefits, but Not Without Some Risk*, GAO-10-611 (Washington, D.C.: June 21, 2010).

[2] American Association of Homes and Services for the Aging (AAHSA) and American Seniors Housing Association (ASHA), *The Assisted Living and Continuing Care Retirement Community State Regulatory Handbook, 2009.*

[3] Florida regulators said that they maintained a spreadsheet containing financial information on CCRCs dating back over a decade and used the data to develop trends of financial ratios for each CCRC.

In: Continuing Care Retirement Communities ISBN 978-1-62100-945-0
Editors: P. G. Moore and L. F. Miller

Chapter 5

TESTIMONY OF KEVIN M. MCCARTY, INSURANCE COMMISSIONER, FLORIDA OFFICE OF INSURANCE REGULATION. HEARING ON "CONTINUING CARE RETIREMENT COMMUNITIES (CCRCS): SECURE RETIREMENT OR RISKY INVESTMENT?"

Good afternoon Mr. Chairman and members of the Committee. My name is Kevin McCarty, Insurance Commissioner with the Florida Office of Insurance Regulation (OIR). Thank you for the invitation to appear before you today to share Florida's experience in regulating continuing care retirement communities (CCRCs). We are pleased the Committee has expressed an interest in these entities, and an interest in helping protect seniors with one of their most important financial and lifestyle decisions.

HISTORY OF CCRC REGULATION IN FLORIDA

In Florida, OIR and the Florida Agency for Health Care Administration (AHCA) regulate CCRCs jointly. AHCA regulates the health care quality of a CCRC while OIR regulates a CCRC's financial solvency, the residency contracts, and the disclosures made to prospective residents. OIR also works in conjunction with the Florida Department of Financial Services (DFS). DFS processes resident complaints not related to the quality of health care and also oversees mediation and arbitration between residents and CCRCs.

Florida Statutes define "continuing care" as furnishing shelter and either nursing care or personal services upon payment of an entrance fee pursuant to a contract. Therefore, OIR does not regulate facilities that do not require an upfront entrance fee.

The first regulation of CCRCs by OIR and its predecessors began in 1953. The original law was limited to the regulation of communities, which exchanged care for a single fixed fee and typically required a resident to assign all of his or her assets to the community. The law did not apply to facilities charging an entrance fee and a monthly maintenance fee or those with a mutual right of contract termination. Consequently, OIR regulated very few facilities and the regulation of these facilities was minimal. These facilities were known as "Life Care" facilities.

After several high-profile bankruptcies that occurred in Florida and nationally, the regulatory climate for CCRCs evolved. In 1977, the Florida Legislature strengthened statutes governing CCRCs by expanding the definition of continuing care and adding new requirements for CCRCs. The 1977 revision formed the foundation of the current regulatory framework governing CCRCs. However, the failure of several CCRCs in the late 1970s and early 1980s prompted the Florida Legislature to further strengthen the CCRC statute in 1981 and in 1983.

Florida CCRC law has continued to undergo modifications. Most recently the 2010 Florida Legislature opted to increase disclosures to prospective and current residents and to recognize that some residents purchase a CCRC contract as a form of long-term care insurance, intending to delay their occupancy of the facility.

Currently, there are 73 licensed CCRCs in Florida serving approximately 30,000 residents. Most of the growth in the industry in Florida has been from existing CCRCs adding units since the number of licensees has remained consistent over the last decade.

In general, new CCRCs have been entering the market at nearly the same rate as existing CCRCs have surrendered their licenses to become non-CCRC, rental communities. The total revenue reported for Florida CCRCs during 2009 was approximately $1.4 billion.

Residents' Rights

It is important to note that the general population utilizing CCRCs are seniors. The decision to join a CCRC represents a substantial investment of an older person's assets, and Florida takes its responsibility to protect these consumers very seriously. In addition to the regulatory oversight structure of CCRCs discussed below, Florida law recognizes that residents of CCRCs are entitled to dignity and respect. Specifically, a section of Florida law governing CCRCs is entitled, "Residents' rights." This section states, among other things, that a resident of a CCRC may not be denied any civil or legal rights, that they are entitled to live in a safe environment, that they are entitled to be treated with dignity and respect, that they are entitled to present grievances and recommend changes in policies and procedures of the CCRC, and that they are entitled to a copy of the these residents' rights.

Overview of Regulatory Structure

OIR's regulatory emphasis focuses on four distinct areas:

1) Verifying that CCRC owners and management are reputable and responsible;
2) Ensuring information is properly disclosed to prospective and current residents;
3) Ensuring compliance with licensure requirements; and
4) Providing financial oversight.

CCRC Owners and Management

OIR considers the CCRC's principals to be a key component of the success of a CCRC facility. Prior to approving an application for licensure, Florida Statutes require a CCRC to submit evidence that the facility's owners and management are reputable and of responsible character and that they have sufficient experience to properly operate a CCRC. To make this determination, OIR requires each officer, director, owner and manager of the CCRC to submit a biographical affidavit, a legible fingerprint card, and an investigative report obtained from an independent vendor. These biographical requirements also apply to any new officers, directors or management of existing CCRCs. These rigorous requirements ensure that people of questionable moral character are not in a position to harm Florida residents.

Disclosures to Residents

Another key component of Florida's CCRC regulation is disclosure requirements to residents. Florida Statutes contain a list of items that must be disclosed to prospective residents prior to entering into a continuing care contract. Some of the more significant items include a summary of the facility's ownership interests and its affiliations, plans for expansion, rules and regulations of the facility, the facility's policy concerning admission to and discharge from the various levels of care, a copy of the resident's rights and a summary of the most recent examination report issued by OIR. A copy of the facility's most recent annual report must also be accessible to prospective residents. A CCRC is required to submit a copy of these disclosure documents on an informational basis to OIR prior to their use.

Florida Statutes also require a number of disclosures in the residency contracts. Each contract must be filed with and approved by OIR prior to its use to ensure that all required disclosures are contained in the contract, the contract meets statutory requirements for items such as refunds provisions, and to ensure the contract is written in plain language.

Florida Statutes require additional items to be disclosed to existing residents on an on-going basis. For example, existing residents are entitled to inspect the facility's annual financial reports and audited financial statements and receive 60-day advance notice of any changes in fees and services. Management is also required to conduct quarterly meetings with residents to discuss items of concern including reasons for fee increases.

To ensure that CCRCs comply with these disclosure requirements, OIR conducts examinations of each facility at least every three years unless they are accredited by an accreditation agency such as Commission for Accreditation of Rehabilitation Facilities-Continuing Care Accreditation Commission (CARF-CCAR). Accredited CCRCs are required to be examined at least once every five years. Currently, 19 of Florida's 73 CCRC facilities are accredited through CARF-CCAC. Florida Statutes also allow OIR to conduct an examination of a facility at any time on a discretionary basis.

LICENSURE REQUIREMENTS

The third emphasis of Florida's CCRC regulation concerns licensure requirements. For example, one of the licensure requirements is that a prospective CCRC must provide evidence of demand for a new facility. Since the viability of a CCRC is primarily governed by occupancy, it is imperative that a CCRC demonstrate sufficient demand for a facility prior to placing the residents' funds at risk. Florida accomplishes this objective by requiring a prospective CCRC to submit a feasibility study with its application for licensure, which follows a two-step application process, and through the escrowing of residents' entrance fees.

A CCRC first obtains a Provisional Certificate of Authority (PCOA) which allows the CCRC to market the facility and collect reservation deposits equal to at least 10% of each entrance fee. A CCRC is prohibited from beginning construction of the facility while under a PCOA. During the PCOA period, prospective residents' deposits are 100% escrowed.

To obtain a full Certificate of Authority (COA), a CCRC must collect a reservation deposit on a minimum of 50% of the independent living units, and submit a second feasibility study -- this one being from an independent consultant. In addition, the CCRC must prove the CCRC has secured financing for the project. OIR has found these requirements to be very important as many projects that have failed in Florida did so during the PCOA phase; these failures were primarily due to the CCRC's failing to meet the 50% reservation requirement. As a result, these facilities were halted prior to construction and the residents received full refunds.

If a facility does obtain the necessary deposits, OIR authorizes the CCRC to begin construction. Under a COA, a CCRC is allowed to access 25% of residents' deposits and entrance fees. The CCRC must maintain the remaining 75% of residents' deposits and entrance fees in escrow to reduce the financial risk to residents until the CCRC demonstrates the facility has a likelihood of success. To obtain release of the remaining initial entrance fees, a CCRC must provide evidence to OIR that the facility is constructed, a certificate of occupancy has been issued, and 70% of the independent living units are paid-in-full. In addition, CCRCs must show statutory reserve requirements have been met and an independent consultant certifies that there have been no material adverse changes with regard to the feasibility study that was submitted with the COA application. After the release of initial entrance fees has occurred, a facility is required to escrow entrance fees for seven days during Florida's rescission period and escrow all wait list deposits which are over $1,500.

FINANCIAL OVERSIGHT

Another critical area of Florida's regulatory emphasis is financial oversight. Each facility is required to file with OIR an annual financial report, audited financial statements and a minimum liquid reserve calculation. Facilities are also required to file quarterly financial reports unless they are accredited. OIR has maintained the financial information from annual reports filed since 1990 and quarterly financial information since 1996.

OIR has used this information to construct spreadsheets that calculate a series of financial ratios to assist OIR in determining the financial viability of a facility. These ratios address a facility's profitability, liquidity, debt levels and occupancy. OIR then uses the ratios and its historical data to analyze the financial trends of a facility to determine whether OIR should take any action in regards to that facility. OIR may require a facility that is experiencing declining financial trends to submit more frequent reports for closer monitoring or OIR may require the CCRC to submit a corrective action plan to address the issues causing the financial problems. A facility with more significant problems may become subject to administrative supervision where an OIR designee oversees the operations of the facility, or a facility may ultimately have its COA suspended.

A CCRC with a suspended COA is restricted from finalizing new residency contracts. A facility that experiences severe problems may have its license revoked or it may be placed into Rehabilitation with DFS pursuant to a court order. Another option for assisting troubled CCRCs in Florida is to refer the facility to the Florida Continuing Care Advisory Council. The Advisory Council consists of three CCRC residents, three CCRC Executive Directors and four professionals familiar with the CCRC industry. The Advisory Council is charged with acting in an advisory role to OIR and assisting with any corrective action plan, rehabilitation or cessation of business plan of a CCRC upon the request of OIR.

In the unfortunate event that a facility is liquidated, Florida Statutes contain provisions to assist residents financially to relocate to other facilities. This process includes DFS becoming a creditor of the facility or through an assessment levied on other CCRCs. Fortunately, this has been a rare event and has not occurred in almost 20 years.

Another important part of financial solvency is each facility's minimum liquid reserve (MLR) which is held in an escrow account. The MLR can be used by the CCRC with OIR approval in an emergency or by DFS if the facility is in rehabilitation as Florida does not have a guaranty fund for CCRCs.

Each facility's MLR consists of a debt service reserve equal to one year of debt service payments, an operating reserve equal to 15% of annual operating expenses, and a renewal and replacement reserve which is equal to 15% of the lesser of annual operating expenses and accumulated depreciation. The operating reserve and renewal and replacement reserve are required to be unencumbered. OIR assists facilities to properly calculate their reserve requirements and then monitors the escrow accounts to ensure that the facility maintains adequate reserve funding.

In addition to emergency funding, the renewal and replacement reserve can serve as a source of inexpensive financing for facilities since the CCRC can access a portion of the renewal and replacement reserve each year to fund capital expenditures. The withdrawals are then required to be repaid in equal installments over a 36 month period.

OIR conducts its financial oversight by assigning each CCRC to one of four CCRC examiners who are responsible for their CCRCs. It is this examiner that reviews and analyzes the financial reports and ensures that a CCRC's reserves are adequately funded. In addition, the examiner reviews any new financing documents such as loan agreements, reviews and approves the escrow agreements that govern the reserve and entrance fee accounts, reviews the CCRC's investments to ensure that they comply with diversification requirements, reviews management agreements, reviews and approves any acquisition filings if a CCRC is acquired, maintains the public records for each facility and serves as a point of contact for any questions from OIR's field auditors, the public or from the CCRC. The CCRC section supervisor provides oversight of the four CCRC examiners and also performs secondary reviews of all financial reports of CCRCs that are deemed to have a higher priority level usually as a result of some financial difficulties.

Regulatory Outreach

OIR receives information from various sources concerning regulatory problems or concerns about CCRCs. For example, each year OIR hosts a meeting of the Advisory Council to discuss industry trends, issues and the regulatory environment. The residents and Executive Directors on the Advisory Council are frank in giving their opinions of areas where OIR should focus its resources. In addition, during each on-site examination, the examiner meets with the President or Chair of the facility's residents' council to discuss any resident concerns. Furthermore, OIR maintains good relations and frequent contact with an industry association that represents many of the Florida CCRC residents (Florida Life Care Residents Association) and an industry association that represents many of the Florida CCRCs (Florida Homes and Services for the Aging). These associations often bring the concerns of their constituents to our attention.

CCRC Trends

CCRCs have continued to evolve to adapt to the changing needs of seniors. Over the last ten years Florida has seen a significant increase in the quantity and quality of services that CCRCs offer to their residents both for the convenience of residents and to obtain additional sources of revenue. For example, several CCRCs in Florida have opened their own home health care agency on campus. The resident receives the benefit of being able to live independently for a longer period of time rather than having to move to the facility's assisted living or skilled nursing units. The resident also gains the benefit of receiving services from a familiar person on campus rather than from a stranger with an outside agency. In turn, the facility gains an additional source of revenue. The facility also may use this program as a marketing tool if they provide the extra services to individuals outside the facility. We have also seen an increase in the number of CCRCs operating their own pharmacies which also provides more convenience to the resident while providing additional revenue for the CCRC.

Another new development in Florida is the "CCRC at Home" concept that may also be characterized as a "CCRC without walls." The main difference between a "CCRC at Home" and a traditional CCRC is that the resident's independent living occurs in his or her own home rather than at an independent living unit at the facility. Therefore, a "CCRC at Home" resident eventually moves to the facility when he or she needs assisted living or skilled nursing services rather than when the residency contract has been signed. As a result, the resident typically pays a much smaller entrance fee than if he or she immediately moved into an independent living unit at the facility.

OIR has received requests from CCRCs that wish to add a "CCRC at Home" program to their existing facilities to generate more revenue. Florida also has a proposed facility that, if successful, will consist mostly of "CCRC at Home" residents. This CCRC proposed this model in response to the poor real estate market resulting in potential residents being unable to sell their homes -- the proceeds of which are typically used to pay the entrance fee due when the residency contract is signed.

CONCLUSION

It has been almost 20 years since a CCRC has failed in Florida, which is perhaps the greatest testament to the success of Florida's regulatory framework. (The residents affected were successfully moved to other facilities.) With that being stated, several Florida CCRC facilities have experienced financial difficulties in recent years, which is partially due to the economy, and more specifically, the depressed housing market. The housing market is especially critical as many residents need to sell their current homes (at reasonable prices) to be able to pay the entrance fees required by a CCRC facility.

OIR continues to monitor several trends in the CCRC industry as these entities adapt to changing economic circumstances. Some of these trends may be favorable, including an expansion of services that will help generate additional revenue, and add to the diversification of CCRC revenue, which will add to these entities' financial stability.

In: Continuing Care Retirement Communities ISBN 978-1-62100-945-0
Editors: P. G. Moore and L. F. Miller

Chapter 6

Testimony of Professor Katherine C. Pearson, Pennsylvania State University. Hearing on "Continuing Care Retirement Communities (CCRCs): Secure Retirement or Risky Investment?"

I am pleased to be invited to speak to the Senate Special Committee on Aging and to have this opportunity to share observations based on several years of research and consultation with residents of Continuing Care Retirement Communities (CCRCs) and Life Care Communities (LFCs) in Pennsylvania and elsewhere in the United States. Thank you.

I am a law professor who focuses on law and aging policy and I am the educational director of Penn State University's Elder Law and Consumer Protection Clinic. Recently, relevant to this topic, I was a visiting scholar at Oregon State University's Gerontology and Family Studies program.

During the last dozen years, I have had multiple opportunities to tour CCRC and LFC sites; to read voluminous marketing materials, application forms and contracts; to review several different state regulatory schemes; and to meet with operators and lawyers for CCRCs and LFCs. Most importantly, I have had frequent opportunities to hear from residents about their experiences and their concerns. My testimony here is based on the legal and policy issues that I perceive, from my perspective in listening to the concerns of residents.

I am a supporter of this form of long-range planning and long-term care. For many thousands of people, CCRCs and LFCs provide an active and supportive environment, with essential flexibility in both housing and care arrangements.

Well-run operations enhance quality of life and make living long a pleasure. One key to success of such operations is the extent to which they can provide predictability about the future. Peace of mind, particularly in later years, is an important goal, and a recognized marketing concept within the industry.

I. Background for CCRC Regulation

I remember hearing the comments of John Erickson, until recently the head of one of the largest CCRC operations in the country, when he was asked in a televised interview about whether he had competitors in the business. He said, in effect, that the greatest challenge he faced was the unwillingness of people to think early enough about retirement living options, especially about what he called the "second half" of retirement, where personal care needs often increase, even for those in good health. I agree with Mr. Erickson on this point; it is tempting to view elder years from the perspective of an ostrich, with our collective heads stuck firmly in the sand.

At the same time, my research makes me realize that some CCRCs and LFCs have succumbed to ostrich-like temptations of their own, as have some state regulators. This format of collective living -- where retirees often commit their life savings to payment of large entrance fees or hefty future monthly fees, in exchange for promises about housing and services for the rest of their lives -- has existed for decades if not centuries. However, the concept first attracted serious public regulatory attention in the 1980s. Notable failures of communities made residents realize that promises can be illusory and the end-of-life consequences particularly disturbing.

Beginning in the 1980s, many states responded by enacting CCRC-specific regulatory schemes that impose licensing standards, often with rules for financial operations. The financial rules often incorporate one or more of three major themes:

First, mandatory "disclosures" to prospective and actual residents,

Second, mandatory minimum financing terms, such as rules for handling of lump-sum payments (sometimes called entrance fees) and requirements for operating reserves, and/or

Third, legal sanctions for certain prohibited conduct, such as misleading, deceptive or fraudulent business practices.

In addition, some state laws address a *fourth* theme, incorporating lessons learned during the legal reform movements of the nursing home industry, by recognizing and adopting specific legal rights for CCRC residents. CCRC residents are active, engaged adults. Many value the right to organize and participate actively in the governance of their village-like communities. Residents frequently seek to exercise their rights in connection with financial decisions and business practices that affect their daily lives and their investments in the community. While some states recognize specific rights for residents, this is the least developed area of regulation, in my opinion.

By my count, more than 30 states have enacted regulations in some form for CCRC operations. I have attached a chart of state statutes, including notes about recent amendments. There are relatively few cases that are reported; litigation of a CCRC resident's right issue is usually cost prohibitive -- and more importantly -- energy depleting for older adults.

The 1990s appeared to be a decade of relative stability and gradual but steady growth of the CCRC industry. By the late 1990s, states had reached what might be called the "teenage" years of CCRC regulation, just as the nation's overall economy seemed to permit any high-flying scheme the chance for immediate success, no matter how much leveraging or debt was involved. At the same time, there were subtle and not- so-subtle shifts within the CCRC industry.

My research suggests that many states did not keep abreast with changes in the industry. Residents are aware of the challenges within the industry and, in some cases, have tried to communicate with regulators. But frequently there is no effective way for residents to raise concerns.

II. The Importance of Resident Voices in CCRCs

About five years ago, a group of residents of a CCRC asked me for a referral for experienced advice about their concerns about an expansion plan at their CCRC. They believed that the plan was unsound, and they impressed me with the sophistication of their reasoning. CCRC residents are often a vital group, with a host of specialized backgrounds. In this instance, the group had residents with skills at crunching numbers and the outcome of their analysis was not satisfactory to them. Attempts to communicate with the management of their CCRC had not been successful. I asked whether they had talked to the state department in charge of CCRC regulation and I learned they had tried to do so, but that they had received no substantive assistance.

That intrigued me, and eventually I tried the same, with the same lack of response to my inquiry about CCRCS operating in the state. I sought information about whether there had been any failures, whether there were any facilities with complaints about financial problems or whether the department was aware of other significant management concerns at CCRCs within the state. I was told, bluntly, that the regulatory scheme required "only" disclosures and not state assessment of the financial health of licensed CCRCs.

I went to view the annual reports filed by CCRCs with that state department and discovered that the public reports were nicely stacked. As far as I could tell, they had never been opened. Since then, I have spoken to other residents and to other regulators. In some instances I have heard regulators report that they do "take action" if they receive notice of financial problems in a CCRC, and one regulator reported that he felt the work of his office had prevented bankruptcies. The latter point sounded particularly positive. I became concerned, however, when I realized that there was no system for tracing complaints and no public reporting of actions taken. It was impossible to determine what factors were contributing to any problems. Residents wanted information so that they could compare their own institution with the success or failure of others. But, there was no systemic information available from the state, even though the state was collecting relevant data.

I wrote a short article in 2006, because I was concerned even then that we were operating like proverbial ostriches, ignoring available evidence of good or less-than good CCRC operations, while we buried our heads in the sand and said "the industry looks healthy from here." In 2006, I wrote that it "seems important to keep a watchful eye for key markers of a stable or unstable industry in light of the apparent sudden growth in CCRCs."

In 2010, we are still in need of that information and we have new reasons to appreciate the absence of the information.

I believe that many – and I hope all – CCRCs will emerge from this challenging economic time intact. I hope I am wrong in my concern that some additional CCRCs will fail, or be drastically restructured to avoid failure. My concern, during this challenging time, is that both current residents and prospective residents need information, information that is not merely stacked in dusty shelves in state offices, but that is read and synthesized and reported candidly, so that current and future residents can make appropriate decisions about their end-of-life investments in CCRCs.

I believe that some states are recognizing the need for more proactive approaches to regulatory assessment. Research discloses that at least seven states have amended their regulations since the financial crisis hit, and I have heard from other states considering changes. For example, Oregon has amended its CCRC law to require greater disclosure of the identities of persons who have direct or indirect ownership or beneficial interests in CCRCs within the state and to require resident representation on the governing boards of CCRCs. *See* Enrolled House Bill 2138, 2009 Oregon Laws Chap. 201, amending Oregon Rev. Stat. §§ 101.010-101.160, effective January 1, 2010.

In reviewing submissions filed with the bankruptcy court in Texas during the Erickson Retirement Communities' bankruptcy case, I have seen a host of objections by non-resident creditors and relatively little from residents themselves. The lack of resident objections is potentially a positive sign as that particular empire emerges from reorganization with new owners. But I also know from years of listening to residents, that some are fearful of speaking out unless they feel someone will listen seriously to their concerns. They fear that they will be shunned, encouraged to leave their homes, or subjected to other negative response if they talk about what they perceive as problems when outside of their campus walls.

State regulators can do a better job of making it safe for residents to speak, and can encourage them to speak while the problems are still solvable. The nation's nursing home industry was changed dramatically, for the better, by adoption of a national bill of residents' rights. *See* 42 U.S.C.A. § 1396r (c). I believe that a national bill of rights for residents in Continuing Care Retirement Communities is also merited, with a goal of providing residents more effective voices, including greater access to transparent financial information. The nursing home bill of rights was predicated on physical or mental vulnerability of residents. With residents at CCRCs, the concern is financial vulnerability in an older population, people who have limited energy and time.

III. Challenges Arising from CCRC Industry Developments

I believe that we must recognize that the CCRC industry is indeed a national industry, even though many CCRCS are still run as individual operations. Residents (and prospective residents) across the nation want more information about financial decisions that affect their communities. There are several key developments that concern residents across the nation.

First, although religious and fraternal organizations continue to have high-profile positions within the CCRC industry, in some instances the "church" or "lodge" in question has little involvement in the daily operation of the facilities. Some non-profits distance themselves from management decisions, decisions that have financial impact on residents. This was once an industry of mostly nonprofit operation facilities managed by their own staffs, and certainly there are many CCRCs that are entirely locally owned and operated. I perceive a trend, however, toward non-profit "affiliation" of facilities. Ownership is still in the hands of non-profits, but management is increasingly "contracted out," and in the hands of management companies (which are often for-profit companies). Residents indicate to me that they would like greater accountability from nonprofit affiliates for the management issues *and* financial operations of their facilities.

Second, for-profit companies in some instances have recognized the benefit of non-profit structures and have created elaborate tiers of for-profit and not-for-profit companies, including development companies, ownership companies, and management companies. These are often tied together with contracts that permit substantial profits to be harvested. Financial instability of any component of these systems affects the overall system. This trend poses unique challenges for anyone attempting to determine financial soundness and accountability. Residents indicate to me that they are often unable to pierce the veils of elaborate structures to get information from the people with the power to make key financial decisions.

Third, residents are concerned about trends in taxation that affect their communities, a concern that is undoubtedly shared by the operators of CCRCs. While not strictly speaking a residents' rights issue, I believe that the soundness of the industry may depend on better guidelines for what will or will not qualify for non-profit consideration in the operation of CCRCs. Residents should not be hit with bad news after their investment decisions are already made. This is a challenge for states (and local taxation authorities), to coordinate their tax collection goals with other regulatory goals for the industry, while still fostering a climate that supports sound growth of a valuable industry.

Finally, the boom in the real estate market that allowed many to reap substantial increases in value from the sales of their homes coincided with abundant creativity and expansion on the part of the CCRC developers. For example, as recently as May 2008, one CEO of a CCRC community operation predicted that his then-current empire, with 20 facilities serving 22,000 residents in 12 states, would grow in the "next couple of years" to serve more than 50,000 residents. This was an interstate operation, even though it had state-specific legal structures. As you may be aware, it was John Erickson who made that prediction, less than 18 months before his communities filed for protection and reorganization under the bankruptcy laws. Erickson Retirement Communities is probably a dramatic example of a uniquely complex structure, but my sense is that other facilities have been moving in the direction of complexity, sometimes driven by the need for more cash or resources to stay solvent. We are seeing, and I believe will continue to see, CCRCs consolidating or joining together, and thus creating more co-dependent entities.

One couple expressed their concern during Erickson Communities bankruptcy case about fees paid to one facility that were used for construction of apartments in other Erickson facilities. They were concerned because they did not know about the leveraging until after the bankruptcy case had been filed. *See* Document 354, Erickson Retirement Communities et al, Case No. 09-037010, U.S. Bankruptcy Court, Northern District of Texas.

Whatever the reasons for the increasing complexity of the structures, it seems wise to recognize that increased complexity contributes to the need for regular reassessment of the industry. Financial decisions in one CCRC unit potentially affect the financial stability of other units within that same ownership group, and ownership can cross state lines. Regulators need to think beyond the borders of a single CCRC campus and beyond the borders of a single state system of regulation. National guidelines are needed. I am aware that the industry itself is preparing new "best practice" guidelines. That is very encouraging; however, I believe this does not eliminate the need for public regulation.

Many in financial circles have had to reconsider their exuberance in predictions. We need to recognize that difficult financial circumstances will not be cured by punitive measures, but also, that the challenging financial climate for CCRCs should not be viewed as an excuse for non-regulation. It is not satisfactory to residents when someone says, "the CCRC industry is too complex" or "too sophisticated" to permit effective state or federal regulation. We need sophisticated regulatory professionals who can and will listen to residents.

IV. A National Bill of Rights for CCRC Residents

The CCRC industry should not be surprised or even upset about federal inquiry into the CCRC industry and the concern for greater financial accountability. The regulation of CCRCs, even those with financial ties that cross state borders, has been largely a function of state regulators. But the industry benefited when Congress adopted federal legislation to assist CCRCs, tied to internal financing questions. In 2005, Congress amended the Medicare and Medicaid laws to require residents at Continuing Care Retirement Communities to spend declared resources before applying for Medicaid for nursing-care needs, thus potentially limiting the healthier spouse's use of the couple's savings. *See* Deficit Reduction Act of 2005, Pub. L. No. 109-171, 2006 Stat. 1932, codified as 42 U.S.C.A. § 1396r (c) (5) (B) (v). *See also* 42 U.S.C.A. §1396p. Thus, CCRC owners have already benefitted from federal regulation.

I am aware that there is little appetite for regulation that will cost additional money to implement. Therefore, with my testimony here I am focusing on a single recommendation, and I believe it is cost efficient, although not cost free to implement properly. I recommend providing residents of CCRCs with a national set of threshold rights, a national bill of CCRC resident rights, geared to their particular concerns about financial accountability and transparency in operations. Many CCRCs already provide, by contract, guaranteed rights to residents. The question is whether such rights adequately address the concerns of residents who want greater financial accountability.

In conclusion, just as the CCRC industry benefitted from federal legislation to address financial concerns, so it is reasonable to expect residents – voters – to be given similar consideration. I believe the first important step is a national bill of rights for residents of Continuing Care Retirement Communities. Providing a national base-line for recognition of the voices of CCRC residents will encourage states and state regulators to work together, will encourage the industry's best practice guidelines to be nationalized, and will help residents enjoy CCRCs for many years to come.

Continuing Care Retirement Community (CCRC& LFC) Statutes – 50 State Survey (updated 7/15/2010)				
State	**Statute**	**Cases of Interest**	**Last amended**	**Amendments added**
Alabama				
Alaska				
Arizona				
Arkansas	Continuing Care Provider Registration Act, ARK. CODE ANN. §§ 23-93-101 to 23-93-114.		2003 & 2009.	Technical changes.
California	CAL. HEALTH & SAFETY CODE § § 1770-1793.84.	Matthews v. State, 163 Cal. Rptr. 741 (Cal. Ct. App. 1980) (CCRC debtor lacked standing to assert claim that state failed to revoke license when debtor failed to maintain statutory reserve levels).	Minor amendment in 2009.	Indicates that no reimbursement charges are required by this act.
Colorado	COLO. REV. STAT. § 10-16-413.5 (slight application to CCRCs).		Effective 1999.	
Connecticut	Management of Continuing Care Facilities, CONN. GEN. STAT. §§ 17b- 520 to 1 7b-549.		Amended 2008 & 2009.	2008: clarified application to in- home services; 2009: Technical changes.
Delaware				
Florida	FLA. STAT. §§ 651.011 to 651.134.	Clearwater Land Co. v. Koepp, 778 So.2d 1022 (Fla. Dist. Ct. App. 2000) (residents could convert "free" nursing center care into home care services on the basis of the daily charges for nursing home care, not assisted living care).	Amended 2010.	Provided further direction for annual reports; provided for non-refundable escrow fees; clarified rights to rescind residency contract; strengthened "residents' council".

(Continued)

Continuing Care Retirement Community (CCRC& LFC) Statutes – 50 State Survey (updated 7/15/2010)				
State	**Statute**	**Cases of Interest**	**Last amended**	**Amendments added**
Georgia	GA. CODE ANN. § 31-6-47; Ga. Code Ann. sec. 33-45-1 to 33-45-12.		Effective 1990.	
Hawaii	HAW. REV. STAT. § 431:10H-219.		Enacted 1999.	
Idaho	Idaho Continuing-Care Disclosure Act, IDAHO CODE ANN. §§ 26-3701 to 26-3715.		Enacted 2005.	
Illinois	20 ILL. COMP. STAT. 3960/12.2 (permits State Board to collect fees from CCRCs).		Enacted 1995.	
Indiana	IND. CODE§§ 23-2-4-1 to 23-2-4-24.		Amended 2009.	Rewrote significant portions (largely definitions and scope).
Iowa				
Kansas				
Kentucky	KY. REV. STAT. ANN. §§ 216B.015, 216B.040, 216B.330-216B.339.		Amended 2007.	Changed name of state agency to which certain reports are submitted.
Louisiana	Louisiana Continuing Care Provider Registration and Disclosure Act, LA. REV. STAT. ANN. §§ 51:2171-51:2188.		Enacted 1987, portions amended in 1989.	Minor textual revision.
Maine	Continuing Care Retirement Communities, ME. REV. STAT. ANN. tit. 24-A §§ 6201-6228.		Portions amended in 2003.	Minor textual revision.

Continuing Care Retirement Community (CCRC& LFC) Statutes – 50 State Survey (updated 7/15/2010)				
State	**Statute**	**Cases of Interest**	**Last amended**	**Amendments added**
Maryland	MD. CODE ANN., HUM. SERV. §§ 10- 401 to 10-499.		Enacted 2007.	
Massachusetts	MASS. GEN. LAWS. *ch*. 93 § 76.		Amended 1996.	Added additional provisions for "long term care services" and other continuing care facilities.
Michigan				
Minnesota	Continuing Care Facility Disclosure and Rehabilitation Act, MINN. STAT. §§ 80D.01-80D.20.		Amended 1981.	
Mississippi				
Missouri	MO. REV. STAT. § 198.048 (brief treatment of CCRCs).		Enacted 1984.	
Montana				
Nebraska				
Nevada				
New Hampshire	N.H. REV. STAT. ANN. § § 420-D: 1 to 420-D:27.		Amended 2010.	Significant changes indicated within NEW HAMPSHIRE 2010 SESSION LAWS 2010 REGULAR SESSION Ch. 144
New Jersey	Continuing Care Retirement Community Regulation and Disclosure Act, N.J. STAT. ANN. § § 52:27D-330 to 52:27D-360.	Seabrook Village v. Murphy, 853 A.2d 280 (N.J. Super. Ct. App. Div. 2004) (resident discharged from continuing care facility has a right to a hearing, and discharge must be based upon "just cause").	Enacted 1986.	

(Continued)

Continuing Care Retirement Community (CCRC& LFC) Statutes – 50 State Survey (updated 7/15/2010)				
State	**Statute**	**Cases of Interest**	**Last amended**	**Amendments added**
New Mexico				
New York	Continuing Care Retirement Communities, N.Y. PUB. HEALTH LAW§§ 4600-4624; A-Fee-ForService Continuing Care Retirement Communities Demonstration Program, N.Y. PUB. HEALTH LAW§§ 4650-4676.		Amended 2003.	Minor additions.
North Carolina	Continuing Care Retirement Communities, N.C. GEN. STAT. §§ 58-64-1 to 58-64-85.		Amended 2003.	Interchanged terms.
North Dakota				
Ohio	OHIO REV. CODE ANN. § § 173.13, 173.42.		No recent amendments.	
Oklahoma				
Oregon	Continuing Care Retirement Community Provider Registration Act, OR. REV. STAT. § § 101.010-101.160.		Amended 2009.	Permits establishment of Resident Councils; mandates registration, disclosure, and reporting to state.
Pennsyl-vania	Continuing-Care Provider Registration and Disclosure Act, 40 PA. STAT. ANN.§§3201-3225.	Moravian Manors v. Commonwealth, 521 A.2d 524 (Pa. Commw. Ct. 1987) (court interpreted Continuing-Care Provider law in determining operation was a "continuing care provider").	No recent amendments.	

Continuing Care Retirement Community (CCRC& LFC) Statutes – 50 State Survey (updated 7/15/2010)				
State	**Statute**	**Cases of Interest**	**Last amended**	**Amendments added**
Rhode Island				
South Carolina	State Continuing Care Retirement Community Act, S.C. CODE ANN. §§ 37-11-10 through 37-11-140.		Amended 2000.	Limited scope of act.
South Dakota				
Tennessee				
Texas	Texas Continuing Care and Disclosure and Rehabilitation and Disclosure Act, TEX. HEALTH & SAFETY CODE ANN. §§ 246.001 through 246.117.		Portions amended 1993, 1995.	Altered terms.
Utah				
Vermont	VT. STAT. ANN. tit. 8 §§ 8001-8018.		Amended 2010.	Added further provisions for "Resident assistance fund."
Virginia	VA. CODE ANN. §§ 38.2-4900 to 38.2-4917.		Last amended 2010.	Technical changes.
Washington	State Health Planning and Resource Development Act, WASH. REV. CODE§§ 70.38.015-70.38.920 (sections not limited to CCRCs).		Portions amended 2005.	Added provisions pertaining to record keeping.
West Virginia	Residential Care Communities, W. VA. CODE§§1 6-5N-1 to 16-5N-1 6.		Effective 1997, amended 2005.	Added section for visitation; modified minimum standards.

(Continued)

Continuing Care Retirement Community (CCRC& LFC) Statutes – 50 State Survey (updated 7/15/2010)				
State	**Statute**	**Cases of Interest**	**Last amended**	**Amendments added**
Wisconsin	WIS. STAT. §§ 647.01-647.08.		Portions updated in 2004 & 2007.	No significant changes
Wyoming				
West Virginia				
Puerto Rico				
District of Columbia	D.C. CODE § § 44-151.01 through 44- 151.18.		Effective 2005.	

In: Continuing Care Retirement Communities ISBN 978-1-62100-945-0
Editors: P. G. Moore and L. F. Miller

Chapter 7

TESTIMONY OF CHARLES W. PRINE, RESIDENT OF CONCORDIA OF THE SOUTH HILLS CCRC. HEARING ON "CONTINUING CARE RETIREMENT COMMUNITIES (CCRCS): SECURE RETIREMENT OR RISKY INVESTMENT?"

My name is Chuck Prine and I want to thank the Committee for providing this opportunity to explain what happened to me and to my fellow residents at the Covenant at South Hills and to offer some suggestions, based on our experience, which might afford some protection to other seniors considering a move to a CCRC.

Like most of the residents, my wife and I selected this community primarily because of the reputation of its sponsor, B'nai B'rith, which promoted itself as a leading operator of senior-living facilities throughout the United States. It later became apparent that B'nai B'rith's actual experience was primarily in government financed low-income rental facilities and that it had no experience whatsoever in building and operating life- care communities.

Furthermore, B'nai B'rith did not invest a penny of its own money in this venture, but rather set up a fully controlled "non-profit" affiliate, which financed the construction and operation of the multi-purpose building through a bond issue and bank loans. Although they had invested no money, B'nai B'rith's stated plan was to draw out of the financing and operation substantial fees and a share of the "profits". Prior to the start of construction, B'nai B'rith's controlled affiliate, the Covenant, agreed to pay B'nai B'rith Housing, Inc., another affiliate of B'nai B'rith, a development fee of $1,000,000. At the same time, pursuant to a licensing agreement, the Covenant agreed to pay B'nai B'rith Housing a licensing fee equal to 50% of its net income.

Almost from the very start, it became apparent that the community had been misrepresented to us and that Covenant was in trouble. Although a sign at the entrance on opening day advertised that there were only seven apartments still available, the highest occupancy achieved several years later was still 14 units short of capacity and fell off sharply as residents died or moved out and were not replaced. The assisted-living and nursing occupancy rates rarely met expectations. The cost of the building exceeded estimates by several million dollars. Constant repairs were required. Costs of staffing and real estate taxes had been grossly underestimated.

All of the directors of the shell corporation set up by B'nai B'rith to oversee the facility were either B'nai B'rith International directors or employees. However, many of them never set foot in the building and they seemed to hold most of their meetings over the phone with the directors from Chicago, Texas, and Washington, DC. They refused to provide an audience for a meeting with the Residents' Council. They allowed the "escrow" fund of resident deposits to be used to make up for lack of other income to pay various bills. They became delinquent in the payment of real estate taxes and defaulted on their debt service.

Eventually, the bond holders, demanded that B'nai B'rith take some drastic action to solve the problem. B'nai B'rith refused to put any of their funds into the situation. They hid behind their shell corporation and finally agreed to hold a series of auctions. The leading bidder turned out to be an outfit which had lost its license to operate in Pennsylvania because of health-care deficiencies. They also were having licensing problems in other states.

We tried to get the Pennsylvania Insurance Department to intervene. Under a state act passed some 25 years ago, they had the right to step in and appoint a trustee to take over the facility, but the Department refused to take this step. Fortunately, the bidder was unable to obtain adequate financing and the deal fell through. I say fortunately because it later turned out that the bidder ran into major financial trouble which newspaper reports indicate was caused by a sort of Ponzi scheme in which some of the investors in their older projects were being paid high interest rates out of funds obtained from investors in their newest units.

In 2009, the bond holders commenced a mortgage foreclosure action in state court. That action could have resulted in the loss of our homes, our long term care insurance and our deposits. Eventually, we landed in Federal Bankruptcy Court where the bond holders and bank lenders refused to consider any kind of resolution in which the residents would receive a single penny. The Residents' Council and the Unsecured Creditors' Committee did play a role, however, in the selection of a new buyer. Through our efforts, we were able to facilitate an arrangement pursuant to which the new owner agreed to honor our existing residency agreements and our life care contracts, but with the total loss of our deposits.

Based on our experience, I would like to make some recommendations for any legislation which might be considered to protect senior citizens from losing their life savings and their long term care in questionably-financed life-care projects.

1. Every project should require a minimum of 30 per cent of the financing coming from a cash investment of the sponsor-owner organization. The primary purpose should be to provide guaranteed lifetime care for the residents rather than provide a high return for Wall Street lenders.
2. Senior housing facilities, which are financed in part by the use of interest obtained from investment of refundable deposits from residents, should be required to place these funds in a true escrow account held by a trustee with the proviso that the principal could not be utilized for operating expenses or other purposes.
3. The boards of directors of the life-care facilities should include at least 33 per cent residents. In effect, these residents should be players, not just pawns in the game. In the case of the Covenant, our residents could have offered several money-saving operational suggestions if we had been granted an opportunity to be heard.
4. In view of the impending increase in longer-living senior citizens, the need for more facilities providing all phases of continuing health care is evident. There should be in each state a single responsible governing agency *as* opposed to responsibilities split among various state agencies. In Pennsylvania, licenses must be obtained from the Department of Insurance, the Department of Public Health and the Department of Welfare. None of these agencies has total control and they do not have, either individually or collectively, sufficient staff and budget to supervise and regulate the facilities.

Not in any sense to diminish the loss our residents have suffered, I am happy to report that our current residents are very pleased with the operation under our new identification, Concordia of the South Hills, which is owned by Concordia Lutheran Ministries of Pittsburgh. In just a few months of ownership, through implementation of their policies and principles, in consultation with the Residents' Council and the residents, the fiscal and operational status of the facility has greatly improved. More than twenty units have been leased to new residents during the first few months of Concordia's ownership. During the last two years of B'nai B'rith's control, only one unit was rented to a new resident. If time allows, I would be pleased to explain in more detail how and why I believe Concordia's modus-operandi will be successful and could be emulated by other life-care facilities.

I welcome your questions.

In: Continuing Care Retirement Communities ISBN 978-1-62100-945-0
Editors: P. G. Moore and L. F. Miller

Chapter 8

TESTIMONY OF DAVID ERICKSON, VICE PRESIDENT FOR LEGAL AFFAIRS, COVENANT RETIREMENT COMMUNITIES. HEARING ON "CONTINUING CARE RETIREMENT COMMUNITIES (CCRCS): SECURE RETIREMENT OR RISKY INVESTMENT?"

Thank You Chairman Kohl, Ranking Member Senator Corker and members of the committee.

My name is David Erickson; I am Vice President for Legal Affairs for Covenant Retirement Communities.

I am here testifying on behalf of the American Association of Homes and Services for the Aging and Covenant Retirement Communities.

Covenant Retirement Communities has 12 CCRCs in 8 states serving over 5,000 residents. Our primary contract has an entry fee and provides for modified life care. Most of our residents chose a 2% per month declining refund option. We also offer 90% refunds, but less than 10% of our residents chose this. We also offer full life care contracts in two communities.

Let me begin by stating that my company, Covenant Retirement Communities, is not connected in any way to Covenant at South Hills. We happen to share the word "covenant" in our name, but beyond that, there is absolutely no connection.

We are, of course, very aware of the significant loss that residents of Covenant at South Hills suffered from failure of that community. That bankruptcy, indeed any bankruptcy in our industry, is something we take very seriously. CCRCs exist for one reason ---- to serve the needs of our residents. Anytime we fail to do that, it is a failure we collectively bear. We deeply regret that it happened.

There are nearly 1,900 CCRCs across the country---the vast majority of which remain strong and financially viable. Notwithstanding the situation at Covenant at South Hills, there are relatively few CCRCs which have faced payment defaults or filed for bankruptcy. And even in those rare cases, the CCRCs have done so without adverse impact to the financial security of their residents—the Covenant at South Hills was clearly an exception. Fortunately, the residents did retain their right to remain at the CCRC under the new ownership and did not have to move.

Without question, the weak economy has impacted CCRCs' occupancies, particularly CCRCs located in regions of the country hardest hit by the decline in housing values. That said, occupancy rates of CCRCs overall continue to exceed those of free-standing assisted living communities, nursing homes, and even free-standing independent living communities. The ability of CCRCs to actually weather the economic storm as well as they have speaks volumes for the strong preference seniors have for a continuum of care lifestyle. Not coincidentally, the typical CCRC reports that resident referrals are the strongest source of leads.

I would like to briefly comment on two reports recently produced by a CCRC task force which I had the honor of chairing. It was formed earlier this year and was comprised of leading experts in CCRC operations, tax-exempt bond financing, and legal and regulatory requirements.

The first report is entitled "Continuing Care Retirement Communities: Suggested Best Practices for CCRC Disclosure and Transparency." The second report is entitled "Today's Continuing Care Retirement Community (CCRC): The strengths of this Popular Senior Living Model, its Stress Points and Challenges... and Its Outlook for Tomorrow". Both of these reports have been supplied to the Committee.

The "Suggested Best Practices for CCRC Disclosure" was developed to help CCRCs in reviewing their individual practices for disclosure; to assist prospective residents in making as informed a decision as possible about moving into a CCRC; and to keep current residents informed. Most CCRCs strongly support disclosure and transparency and routinely disclose a significant amount of information to residents prior to move-in. The

"Suggested Best Practices" publication was simply an effort to provide guidance and document these practices.

The other report prepared by the task force is entitled "Today's Continuing Care Retirement Communities." It presents a historical overview of CCRCs, describes the variety of services offered, and discusses the current financial outlook for CCRCs. This report was thoroughly researched and we believe is an accurate and fair analysis of CCRCs' financial performance and outlook for the future, which we believe is very strong. As shown in this report, CCRCs have evolved over the last decades, diversifying the types of services and amenities they offer in response to growing consumer preferences for choices.

CCRCs are an important option in living arrangements for seniors. Over the decades, CCRCs have successfully offered a continuum of care lifestyle highly desired by seniors. The vast majority are financially stable and provide a style of living which emphasizes healthy aging; have numerous options of living and financial arrangements to meet a variety of consumer preferences; and promote an active and engaged lifestyle. Unlike the housing market or equities market, where large numbers of seniors have had their portfolios affected, the vast majority of CCRCs have provided security and care for seniors who will know where they will live and receive care usually for the rest of their lives. CCRC residents have moved into communities where they have chosen a lifestyle that provides comfort for their families who will not have to worry about what will happen to Mom or Dad as they age. As the "CCRC Story" reports, a common sentiment of CCRCs residents is that they wished they would have moved into the CCRC sooner.

CCRC providers recognize the importance and need for effective state regulatory oversight of CCRCs. But we also believe this regulatory framework has to maintain a balance that provides for adequate consumer protections without unreasonably restricting growth and development of CCRCs. There is certainly a place for reasonable requirements including disclosure requirements, capital reserves and protections of refundable entry fees. However, if these requirements become too prescriptive, expansion of existing CCRCs and development of new ones will be slowed or halted and seniors will lose the opportunity to move into a living environment many clearly prefer. Excessive regulatory restrictions also could prevent CCRCs from offering the varieties of living arrangements that consumers seek.

Similarly, requirements related to the operating and governance structure should be reasonable. For example, many CCRC sponsoring organizations, often not-for-profit religious or fraternal organizations, recognize a need in their local community for the types of services a CCRC provides, but lack the expertise to develop and operate the CCRC. Third party developers and operators fill this need, but that doesn't mean the not-for-profit sponsor isn't an active partner in the operations of the CCRC. In fact, if you look at most of these types of operational structures, you will find an active and involved Board of Trustees.

Thank you for this opportunity to testify on behalf of CCRC providers across this country. We are proud of our long-standing history in serving seniors across this country and stand ready to assist the efforts of this Committee in any way we can. We will continue to work collaboratively with state regulators to support strong and effective state regulations and oversight.

INDEX

A

B

C

D

E

F

G

H

I

L

M

N

O

P

R

S

T

U

V

W